**PRACTICE
MAKES
PERFECT**®

Basic Latin

Basic Latin

Randall Childree, PhD

New York Chicago San Francisco Athens London Madrid
Mexico City Milan New Delhi Singapore Sydney Toronto

3 4 5 6 7 8   QVS/QVS   19 18 17 16 15

ISBN   978-0-07-182141-4
MHID   0-07-182141-4

e-ISBN   978-0-07-182142-1
e-MHID   0-07-182142-2

Library of Congress Control Number 2013947037

McGraw-Hill Education products are available at special quantity discounts to use as premiums and sales promotions or for use in corporate training programs. To contact a representative, please visit the Contact Us pages at www.mhprofessional.com.

This book is printed on acid-free paper.

For my old classmates at the University of Florida:
"It's *flāva*, etc."

Contents

Introduction

Welcome to *Practice Makes Perfect: Basic Latin*! This book includes 170 exercises that are intended to take you from practicing Latin to perfecting it. Everything here has been planned to reinforce what is most useful, based on my experience teaching beginning Latin students.

Students can be intimidated, for example, by the many different forms that Latin words take. This workbook offers straightforward explanations of Latin's declensions and conjugations, and lots of opportunities to practice their forms. Extra emphasis is put on the third-person forms, because they predominate in Latin texts.

Vocabulary is the **sine quā nōn** of language study; if you don't know what the words mean, you just can't do it. So the Latin-English glossary at the back of this book contains almost a thousand words, and the words included have been chosen based on their frequency in the speeches, poems, histories, and plays Latin students are most likely to want to read. The glossary is, in its own right, a useful tool. In addition, as each chapter covers a specific group of words—say, third-declension nouns—there is a list of all of the most frequent words in that group. If you want to make sure that you aren't surprised by any third-declension noun that you ought to know, these lists are a great place to start.

Latin is an incredibly rewarding language to learn. If you can read Latin, you can read works like these:

Cicero's bombastic speeches and intimate letters
Caesar's reputation-boosting war narratives
Vergil's epic tale of the founding of Rome
Catullus and Propertius's startling love poetry
Lucretius's atom-centered explanation of the universe
Ovid's mythological metamorphoses
Suetonius's scandalous accounts of the emperors
Livy and Tacitus's illuminating histories of Rome

Whether you are just starting out, looking for extra help, or wanting to jump-start yourself back into Latin, *Practice Makes Perfect: Basic Latin* will put you in the perfect position to succeed!

The sounds of Latin • Using a dictionary

The alphabet

The alphabet of Latin is made up of the following letters:

a/ā	g	n	t
b	h	o/ō	u/ū/v
c	i/ī	p	x
d	k	q	y/ȳ
e/ē	l	r	z
f	m	s	

LETTER	PRONUNCIATION
a (short vowel)	as in *aqua*
ā (long vowel)	same as the short vowel, but sounded twice as long
b	as in English
c	always hard like *k*, even in Latin words like *Caesar*, *charta*, and *socius*
d	as in English
e (short vowel)	as in *ebony*
ē (long vowel)	as in *wade*
f	as in English
g	always hard as in *gate*, not soft as in *giraffe*
h	as in English
i* (consonant)	as in *year*
i* (short vowel)	as in *trick*
ī* (long vowel)	as in *these*
k†	as in English
l	as in English
m	as in English
n	as in English
o (short vowel)	as in *often*
ō (long vowel)	as in *low*
p	as in English, even in Latin words like *philosophia*
q	always combines with *u* to sound like *kw*
r	as in English, but trilled
s	always hisses as in *sit*, never buzzes as in *miserable*
t	always as in *top*, even in Latin words like *thermae* and *ratiō*

*The letter **i** acts as a consonant before a vowel. The letter **j**, which is merely an ornate form of **i**, did not exist in antiquity.

†The letter **k** is rare.

LETTER	PRONUNCIATION
v* (consonant)	like *w*
u* (short vowel)	as in *put*
ū* (long vowel)	as in *dude*
x	like *ks*
y† (short vowel)	with the mouth in position to say *o*, but saying *u* instead
ȳ† (long vowel)	same as the short vowel, but sounded twice as long
z†	like *ds*

*The letters **u** and **v** are really the same letter, but traditionally, **v** is written for the consonant form.

†The letters **y**, **ȳ**, and **z** are Greek letters and appear only in words that are borrowed from Greek.

Diphthongs

Diphthongs are two vowel sounds blending together in pronunciation. Latin has three common diphthongs (*ae*, *au*, and *oe*) and three that appear in only a few words (*ei*, *eu*, and *ui*).

DIPHTHONG	PRONUNCIATION
ae	as in *aisle*
au	as in *now*
ei	as in *say*
eu	like Latin *e* followed quickly by Latin *u*
oe	as in *boy*
ui	as in *chewy*, but with the vowel sounds run together more quickly

Dividing words into syllables

The syllable is the basic unit of pronunciation. Vowel sounds are the basis of a syllable: a syllable is made up of a vowel sound by itself or a vowel sound in combination with one or more consonant sounds.

Here are rules for dividing a word into syllables:

1. A consonant is attached to a vowel that follows it.

    ho|mi|nis
    vī|tae
    do|mi|nōs

2. If there are two vowels together that don't form a diphthong, the vowels form two separate syllables.

    de|us
    fa|ci|ō

3. If there are two consecutive consonants, the first belongs to the syllable before and the second to the syllable after.

    tem|pus
    noc|tem
    an|nō|rum
    mul|tīs
    om|ni|um

4. If there are more than two consecutive consonants, the first consonant generally belongs to the syllable before, and the rest to the syllable after. Large clusters of consonants are not very common in Latin.

> mon|strā|bat
> pul|chrās
> tem|plum

Accent

The accent in Latin falls on one of the last three syllables, according to the following rules:

1. If the word has only one syllable, the accent is on that syllable.

> et'
> sum'
> vir'

2. If the word has two syllables, the accent is on the second-last syllable.

> fe'|rō
> ma'|nūs
> pa'|ter

3. If the word has three or more syllables, the accent falls on the third-last syllable, unless the second-last syllable contains a long vowel or a diphthong or is a closed syllable (a syllable that ends in a consonant). In these cases, the accent falls on the second-last syllable.

au'|di|ō	BUT	au|dī'|re
a'|gi|mus	BUT	a|gen'|tī
fa'|ci|et	BUT	fa|ci|ē'|mus
rē'|gi|bus	BUT	re|gun'|tur
tem'|po|ris	BUT	a|mā|tō'|ris

EXERCISE
1·1

Practice pronouncing the following syllables.

ba	bā	bō	bi	bu	mus	tur	ās	at	unt	ent	ēs
ōs	īs	bus	hae	hī	ē	ve	vu	vī	iam	iē	et
quī	nū	am	tā	ti	cu	coe	cui	gau	dei	seu	sē
ex	cha	phi	trō	lō	rē						

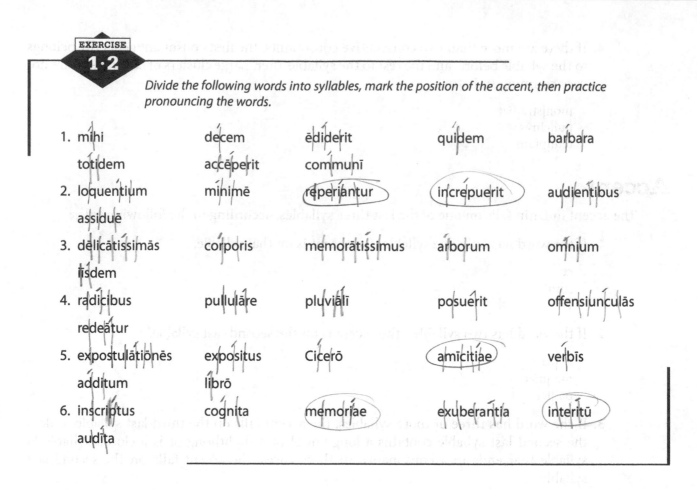

EXERCISE 1·2

Divide the following words into syllables, mark the position of the accent, then practice pronouncing the words.

1. mihi   decem   ēdiderit   quidem   barbara
   totidem   accēperit   commūnī

2. loquentium   minimē   reperiantur   increpuerit   audientibus
   assiduē

3. dēlicātissimās   corporis   memorātissimus   arborum   omnium
   īsdem

4. rādīcibus   pullulāre   pluviālī   posuerit   offensiunculās
   redeātur

5. expostulātiōnēs expositus   Cicerō   amīcitiae   verbīs
   additum   librō

6. inscrīptus   cognita   memoriae   exuberantia   interitū
   audīta

Using a dictionary

Reading Latin sometimes involves looking up a word in a dictionary or glossary, so it's important to know what information the dictionary provides about a word. The three most important categories of words are nouns, verbs, and adjectives.

Nouns

The dictionary entry for a Latin noun has four parts.

1	2	3	4
rex	**rēgis**	*m.*	king

1. Nominative singular form
2. Genitive singular form
3. Gender
4. English meaning

Part 2 is particularly important, because its ending indicates which declension the noun belongs to, and this indicates the noun's form and function.

GENITIVE SINGULAR ENDING	DECLENSION
-ae	FIRST
-ī	SECOND
-is	THIRD
-ūs	FOURTH
-eī/-ēī	FIFTH

Verbs

The dictionary entry for a Latin verb has five parts.

1	2	3	4	5
dīcō	**dīcere**	**dīxī**	**dictum**	to say

1. First principal part
2. Second principal part
3. Third principal part
4. Fourth principal part
5. English meaning

Principal parts provide important information about verbs and verb forms. The first and second principal parts indicate which conjugation a verb belongs to. (There are some irregular verbs, of course, which don't fit into the regular conjugations.)

FIRST PRINCIPAL PART ENDING	SECOND PRINCIPAL PART ENDING	CONJUGATION
-ō	-āre	FIRST
-eō	-ēre	SECOND
-ō	-ere	THIRD
-iō	-ere	THIRD **-IŎ**
-iō	-īre	FOURTH

Adjectives

The dictionary entry for a Latin adjective has either three or four parts. These parts provide the nominative forms of the adjective in each of the grammatical genders—masculine (*m.*), feminine (*f.*), and neuter (*n.*)—and the word's meaning.

1	2	3	4
magnus	**magna**	**magnum**	large, impressive

1	2	3
omnis	**omne**	every, all

The form of the dictionary entry and the number of parts indicate which category the adjective belongs to.

ADJECTIVE ENDINGS	DECLENSION
-us -a -um	FIRST/SECOND
-er -ris -re	THIRD (THREE ENDINGS)
-is -e	THIRD (TWO ENDINGS)
(only one nominative ending, but also gives a genitive form)	THIRD (ONE ENDING)

Identify each of the following words as a noun, verb, or adjective. For each noun or adjective, indicate its declension. For each verb, indicate its conjugation. For some of the words, you may need to consult the glossary at the end of this book.

1. dīcō — _Verb, third, to say_

2. faciō — _verb, third, to face_

λ 3. videō — _"   "   to see_

✗ 4. fēlix — _noun, third, lucky_

^ 5. deus — _noun, fourth, god_

6. rēs — _noun, Fifth, thing_

7. rex — _noun, third, king_

✗ 8. veniō — _verb, third, come_

9. tempus — _noun, 3rd, time_

10. manus — _noun, 4th, hand_

✗ 11. terra — _noun, 4th, land_

12. vir — _noun, 2nd, man_

13. domus — _noun, 4th, house_

14. pars — _adjective, 3rd, part_

15. omnis — _adj, 3, all_

16. urbs — _noun, 3, city_

✗ 17. vocō — _verb, [ ], call_

✗ 18. longus — _adj, [ ], long_

19. fortis — _adj, 3, strong_

20. ācer — _adj, 3, sharp_

Verbs • The present tense of first-, second-, and fourth-conjugation verbs

Verb characteristics

Every verb has certain features that we can use to describe it precisely. These features are called the *characteristics* of the verb. Latin verbs have the following five characteristics:

1. *Person*, which indicates who is performing the action of the verb
2. *Number*, which indicates whether the subject of the verb is singular or plural
3. *Tense*, which indicates when the action of the verb happens
4. *Voice*, which indicates whether the subject is performing or undergoing the action of the verb
5. *Mood*, which indicates the relationship between the action of the verb and reality

Latin encodes all of these characteristics into a verb by using a series of endings added to verbal roots. If you can decode the endings, you can find out all of this information quickly and easily.

This chapter discusses person, number, and one of the tenses. The other tenses, along with voice and mood, are discussed in later chapters.

The present tense

The present tense describes actions as occurring at the present moment. The usual English translation is simply _____s or is _____ing. For example:

amant	*they love / they are loving*
capis	*you take / you are taking*
audīmus	*we hear / we are hearing*

The present tense of Latin verbs is formed by combining the present system root with the active personal endings (with slight adjustments in some forms).

The present system root

To find the present system root of any verb, drop the **-re** ending of the second principal part; what's left is the root. For example:

PRINCIPAL PARTS	PRESENT SYSTEM ROOT
amō, amāre, amāvī, amātum	amāre
habeō, habēre, habuī, habitum	habēre
agō, agere, ēgī, actum	agere
capiō, capere, cēpī, captum	capere
audiō, audīre, audīvī, audītum	audīre

EXERCISE 2·1

Write the present system root of each of the following verbs.

1. petō   _pet_
2. creō   _cre_
3. nesciō   _nes_
4. cōgitō   _cogi_
5. cupiō   _cup_

6. iaceō   _iac_
7. gerō   _ger_
8. discēdō   _disced_
9. tangō   _tang_
10. pugnō   _pugn_

The active personal endings

Latin attaches the active personal endings to the end of the system root to encode two of the verb's characteristics:

1. *Person.* The first person is the speaker, the second person is the person spoken to, and the third person is a person or thing being spoken about.
2. *Number.* There are two numbers: singular (*sg.*) and plural (*pl.*).

Here are the active personal endings:

	SINGULAR		PLURAL	
FIRST PERSON	-ō/-m	*I*	-mus	*we*
SECOND PERSON	-s	*you*	-tis	*you*
THIRD PERSON	-t	*he/she/it*	-nt	*they*

Identify the person and number of each of the following verbs.

1. orant _____
2. bibis _____
3. pereō _____
4. aufertis _____
5. scrībit _____

6. dolet _____
7. dormiunt _____
8. implēmus _____
9. trahō _____
10. crescis _____

If you know how the present system root and the active personal endings work, you can easily form the present tense of any verb of the first, second, or fourth conjugation. Here are charts of example verbs:

First conjugation

amō, amāre, amāvī, amātum *love*

PRESENT SYSTEM ROOT   amā-

	SINGULAR		PLURAL	
FIRST PERSON	amō*	*I love*	amā**mus**	*we love*
SECOND PERSON	amā**s**	*you love*	amā**tis**	*you love*
THIRD PERSON	ama**t**	*he/she/it loves*	ama**nt**	*they love*

Second conjugation

teneō, tenēre, tenuī, tentum *hold*

PRESENT SYSTEM ROOT   tenē-

	SINGULAR		PLURAL	
FIRST PERSON	teneō	*I hold*	tenē**mus**	*we hold*
SECOND PERSON	tenē**s**	*you hold*	tenē**tis**	*you hold*
THIRD PERSON	tene**t**	*he/she/it holds*	tene**nt**	*they hold*

Fourth conjugation

audiō, audīre, audīvī, audītum *hear*

PRESENT SYSTEM ROOT   audī-

	SINGULAR		PLURAL	
FIRST PERSON	audiō	*I hear*	audī**mus**	*we hear*
SECOND PERSON	audī**s**	*you hear*	audī**tis**	*you hear*
THIRD PERSON	audi**t**	*he/she/it hears*	audiu**nt***	*they hear*

---

*There are two exceptions: (1) The **-ā-** of the first-conjugation root is omitted in the first person singular of first-conjugation verbs, and (2) **-u-** is inserted in the third person plural of fourth-conjugation verbs. Notice that for verb forms ending in **-ō**, **-t**, or **-nt**, the vowel at the end of the root becomes short; this is true for all Latin verb forms with these endings.

Keeping the same person, transform each of the following verb forms into its opposite number, singular to plural or plural to singular.

1. praestātis _____
2. fingimus _____
3. moveō _____
4. sentīs _____
5. dēbent _____

6. parant _____
7. imperās _____
8. videt _____
9. valētis _____
10. revocant _____

Give all six forms of the present tense for each of the following verbs.

1. maneō _____
2. audiō _____
3. exerceō _____
4. vigilō _____
5. caveō _____
6. conveniō _____
7. vocō _____
8. certō _____
9. sepeliō _____
10. mūtō _____

Translate each of the following verb forms into English.

1. orant _____
2. bibis _____
3. pereō _____
4. aufertis _____
5. scrībit _____

6. dolet _____
7. dormiunt _____
8. implēmus _____
9. trahō _____
10. crescis _____

Translate each of the following verb phrases into Latin.

1. they equip _____

2. you (*sg.*) discover _____

3. she arrives _____

4. they are slaves _____

5. you (*pl.*) are earning _____

6. you (*sg.*) rule _____

7. it holds _____

8. we are pleasing _____

9. they help _____

10. you (*sg.*) are weeping _____

VOCABULARY

Common first-, second-, and fourth-conjugation verbs

First-conjugation verbs

agitō, agitāre, agitāvī, agitātum	*pursue*
amō, amāre, amāvī, amātum	*love*
appellō, appellāre, appellāvī, appellātum	*call by name*
armō, armāre, armāvī, armātum	*equip*
cantō, cantāre, cantāvī, cantātum	*sing*
celebrō, celebrāre, celebrāvī, celebrātum	*honor*
certō, certāre, certāvī, certātum	*contend*
cessō, cessāre, cessāvī, cessātum	*yield*
cōgitō, cōgitāre, cōgitāvī, cōgitātum	*think*
comparō, comparāre, comparāvī, comparātum	*prepare*
constō, constāre, constitī	*be fixed*
creō, creāre, creāvī, creātum	*create*
cūrō, cūrāre, cūrāvī, cūrātum	*care for*
dēsīderō, dēsīderāre, dēsīderāvī, dēsīderātum	*wish for*
dōnō, dōnāre, dōnāvī, dōnātum	*give as a gift*
errō errāre errāvī errātum	*stray*
existimō, existimāre, existimāvī, existimātum	*estimate*
exspectō, exspectāre, exspectāvī, exspectātum	*await*
ignōrō, ignōrāre, ignōrāvī, ignōrātum	*not know*
imperō, imperāre, imperāvī, imperātum	*order*
indicō, indicāre, indicāvī, indicātum	*point out*
interrogō, interrogāre, interrogāvī, interrogātum	*ask, question*
intrō, intrāre, intrāvī, intrātum	*enter*
iūrō, iūrāre, iūrāvī, iūrātum	*swear*

iuvō, iuvāre, iūvī, iūtum	help
labōrō, labōrāre, labōrāvī, labōrātum	work
laudō, laudāre, laudāvī, laudātum	praise
līberō, līberāre, līberāvī, līberātum	free
mandō, mandāre, mandāvī, mandātum	entrust
memorō, memorāre, memorāvī, memorātum	recall
mūtō, mūtāre, mūtāvī, mūtātum	change
narrō, narrāre, narrāvī, narrātum	tell a story
negō, negāre, negāvī, negātum	say not
nōminō, nōmināre, nōmināvī, nōminātum	name
optō, optāre, optāvī, optātum	wish
ornō, ornāre, ornāvī, ornātum	decorate
ōrō, ōrāre, ōrāvī, ōrātum	ask for
parō, parāre, parāvī, parātum	provide
peccō, peccāre, peccāvī, peccātum	make a mistake
portō, portāre, portāvī, portātum	carry
postulō, postulāre, postulāvī, postulātum	demand
praestō, praestāre, praestitī, praestātum	excel
probō, probāre, probāvī, probātum	approve
properō, properāre, properāvī, properātum	hurry
pugnō, pugnāre, pugnāvī, pugnātum	fight
putō, putāre, putāvī, putātum	think
regnō, regnāre, regnāvī, regnātum	rule
revocō, revocāre, revocāvī, revocātum	call back
rogō, rogāre, rogāvī, rogātum	ask
servō, servāre, servāvī, servātum	save
sonō, sonāre, sonuī, sonitum	make a sound
spērō, spērāre, spērāvī, spērātum	hope
stō, stāre, stetī, statum	stand
superō, superāre, superāvī, superātum	survive, outdo
temptō, temptāre, temptāvī, temptātum	try
vacō, vacāre, vacāvī, vacātum	be idle
vigilō, vigilāre, vigilāvī, vigilātum	stay awake
vocō, vocāre, vocāvī, vocātum	call
volō, volāre, volāvī, volātum	fly

Second-conjugation verbs

appāreō, appārēre, appāruī, appāritum	appear
ardeō, ardēre, arsī	burn
augeō, augēre, auxī, auctum	increase
careō, carēre, caruī, caritum	lack
caveō, cavēre, cāvī, cautum	be careful
contineō, continēre, continuī, contentum	contain
dēbeō, dēbēre, dēbuī, dēbitum	ought to
decet, decēre, decuit	it suits
doceō, docēre, docuī, doctum	teach
doleō, dolēre, doluī, dolitum	suffer
exerceō, exercēre, exercuī, exercitum	train
fleō, flēre, flēvī, flētum	weep
gaudeō, gaudēre, gāvīsus	rejoice
habeō, habēre, habuī, habitum	have
iaceō, iacēre, iacuī, iacitum	lie

impleō, implēre, implēvī, implētum	*fill*
invideō, invidēre, invīdī, invīsum	*envy*
iubeō, iubēre, iussī, iussum	*order*
licet, licēre, licuit	*it is allowed*
maneō, manēre, mansī, mansum	*remain*
mereō, merēre, meruī, meritum	*earn*
misceō, miscēre, miscuī, mixtum	*mix*
moneō, monēre, monuī, monitum	*advise*
moveō, movēre, mōvī, mōtum	*move*
noceō, nocēre, nocuī, nocitum	*harm*
oportet, oportēre, oportuit	*it is proper*
pateō, patēre, patuī	*be open*
placeō, placēre, placuī, placitum	*be pleasing*
praebeō, praebēre, praebuī, praebitum	*offer*
respondeō, respondēre, respondī, responsum	*answer*
retineō, retinēre, retinuī, retentum	*hold back*
rīdeō, rīdēre, rīsī, rīsum	*laugh*
sedeō, sedēre, sēdī, sessum	*sit*
soleō, solēre, solitus	*be accustomed*
studeō, studēre, studuī	*be eager*
sustineō, sustinēre, sustinuī	*support*
taceō, tacēre, tacuī, tacitum	*be quiet*
teneō, tenēre, tenuī, tentum	*hold*
timeō, timēre, timuī	*be afraid*
valeō, valēre, valuī, valitum	*be strong*
videō, vidēre, vīdī, vīsum	*see*

Fourth-conjugation verbs

aperiō, aperīre, aperuī, apertum	*open*
audiō, audīre, audīvī, audītum	*hear*
conveniō, convenīre, convēnī, conventum	*come together, agree*
dormiō, dormīre, dormīvī, dormītum	*sleep*
inveniō, invenīre, invēnī, inventum	*discover*
nesciō, nescīre, nescīvī, nescītum	*not know*
perveniō, pervenīre, pervēnī, perventum	*arrive*
reperiō, reperīre, repperī, repertum	*discover*
sciō, scīre, scīvī, scītum	*know*
sentiō, sentīre, sensī, sensum	*perceive*
sepeliō, sepelīre, sepelīvī, sepultum	*bury*
serviō, servīre, servīvī, servītum	*be a slave*
veniō, venīre, vēnī, ventum	*come*

The present tense of third and third -iō conjugation verbs

The third and third -iō conjugations

The third and third -**iō** conjugations are slightly trickier than the first, second, and fourth conjugations, because the vowel at the end of the present system root is short—not long, as in the first, second, and fourth conjugations. That short root vowel undergoes a weakening when it combines with the personal endings and becomes -**i**-.

Third conjugation

pōnō, pōnere, posuī, positum *put*
PRESENT SYSTEM ROOT   pōne-

	SINGULAR		PLURAL	
FIRST PERSON	pōnō*	*I put*	pōni**mus**	*we put*
SECOND PERSON	pōnis	*you put*	pōni**tis**	*you put*
THIRD PERSON	pōnit	*he/she/it puts*	pōnunt*	*they put*

Third -iō conjugation

capiō, capere, cēpī, captum *take*
PRESENT SYSTEM ROOT   cape-

	SINGULAR		PLURAL	
FIRST PERSON	capiō	*I take*	capi**mus**	*we take*
SECOND PERSON	capis	*you take*	capi**tis**	*you take*
THIRD PERSON	capit	*he/she/it takes*	capiunt*	*they take*

---

*Notice that the weakened **vowel** of the root disappears altogether in the first person singular form of the third conjugation and that -**u**- precedes the personal ending in the third person plural forms.

Identify the person and number of each of the following verbs.

1. impōnit _____
2. addō _____
3. fallitis _____
4. parcitis _____
5. faciō _____

6. surgit _____
7. efficis _____
8. vincō _____
9. permittunt _____
10. induimus _____

Keeping the same person, transform each of the following verb forms into its opposite number, singular to plural or plural to singular.

1. relinquit _____
2. colis _____
3. metuitis _____
4. vertimus _____
5. conspiciunt _____

6. accipiō _____
7. gignimus _____
8. iacit _____
9. intellegit _____
10. currunt _____

Give all six forms of the present tense for each of the following verbs.

1. quaerō _____
2. condō _____
3. legō _____
4. cadō _____
5. praecipiō _____
6. ēligō _____
7. ēripiō _____
8. iungō _____
9. premō _____
10. pergō _____

EXERCISE

3·4

Translate each of the following verb forms into English.

1. pendis _____
2. āmittunt _____
3. fīgitis _____
4. recipis _____
5. cernō _____

6. reddimus _____
7. cēdit _____
8. consulunt _____
9. claudis _____
10. interficiō _____

EXERCISE

3·5

Translate each of the following verb phrases into Latin.

1. you (*sg.*) are composing _____
2. you (*pl.*) pour _____
3. they snatch _____
4. we deceive _____
5. it carries _____
6. you (*pl.*) flow _____
7. I sprinkle _____
8. we are seeking _____
9. you (*pl.*) are stretching _____
10. I begin _____

VOCABULARY

Common third and third -iō conjugation verbs

Third-conjugation verbs

accēdō, accēdere, accessī, accessum	*approach*
accidō, accidere, accidī	*happen*
addō, addere, addidī, additum	*add*
agō, agere, ēgī, actum	*drive, act*
āmitto, āmittere, āmīsī, āmissum	*lose*
ascendō, ascendere, ascendī, ascensum	*climb*
bibō, bibere, bibī	*drink*

cadō, cadere, cecidī, cāsum	*fall*
canō, canere, cecinī, cantum	*sing*
cēdō, cēdere, cessī, cessum	*go, yield*
cernō, cernere, crēvī, crētum	*discern*
cingō, cingere, cinxī, cinctum	*encircle*
claudō, claudere, clausī, clausum	*close*
cognoscō, cognoscere, cognōvī, cognitum	*recognize*
cōgō, cōgere, coēgī, coactum	*compel*
colligō, colligere, collēgī, collectum	*collect*
colō, colere, coluī, cultum	*inhabit, worship*
comedō, comedere, comēdī, comessum	*eat*
committō, committere, commīsī, commissum	*entrust*
compōnō, compōnere, composuī, compositum	*compose*
concēdō, concēdere, concessī, concessum	*give up*
condō, condere, condidī, conditum	*store*
constituō, constituere, constituī, constitūtum	*establish*
consulō, consulere, consuluī, consultum	*take counsel*
contemnō, contemnere, contempsī, contemptum	*condemn*
contingō, contingere, contigī, contactum	*touch*
convertō, convertere, convertī, conversum	*turn over*
crēdō, crēdere, crēdidī, crēditum	*believe*
crescō, crescere, crēvī, crētum	*increase*
currō, currere, cucurrī, cursum	*run*
dēdūcō, dēdūcere, dēduxī, dēductum	*lead down*
dēfendō, dēfendere, dēfendī, dēfensum	*defend*
descendō, descendere, descendī, descensum	*climb down*
dīcō, dīcere, dixī, dictum	*say*
dīligō, dīligere, dīlexī, dīlectum	*esteem*
dīmittō, dīmittere, dīmīsī, dīmissum	*send away*
dīrigō, dīrigere, dīrexī, dīrectum	*guide*
discēdō, discēdere, discessī, discessum	*leave*
discō, discere, didicī	*learn*
dīvidō, dīvidere, dīvīsī, dīvīsum	*divide*
dūcō, dūcere, duxī, ductum	*lead*
ēligō, ēligere, ēlēgī, ēlectum	*choose*
ēvādō, ēvādere, ēvāsī, ēvāsum	*escape*
fallō, fallere, fefellī, falsum	*deceive*
fīgō, fīgere, fixī, fixum	*fasten*
fingō, fingere, finxī, fictum	*devise*
fluō, fluere, fluxī, fluxum	*flow*
frangō, frangere, frēgī, fractum	*break*
fundō, fundere, fūdī, fūsum	*pour*
gerō, gerere, gessī, gestum	*carry*
gignō, gignere, genuī, genitum	*give birth to*
impōnō, impōnere, imposuī, impositum	*put onto*
induō, induere, induī, indūtum	*put on*
instituō, instituere, instituī, institūtum	*establish*
instruō, instruere, instruxī, instructum	*build*
intellegō, intellegere, intellexī, intellectum	*understand*
intendō, intendere, intendī, intentum	*strain*
iungō, iungere, iunxī, iunctum	*join*
legō, legere, lēgī, lectum	*read*

linquō, linquere, līquī	*abandon*
lūdō, lūdere, lūsī, lūsum	*play*
metuō, metuere, metuī, metūtum	*fear*
mittō, mittere, mīsī, missum	*send*
neglegō, neglegere, neglexī, neglectum	*disregard*
noscō, noscere, nōvī, nōtum	*know*
occīdō, occīdere, occīdī, occīsum	*kill*
ostendō, ostendere, ostendī, ostensum	*show*
pandō, pandere, pandī, passum	*spread*
parcō, parcere, pepercī	*spare*
pendō, pendere, pependī, pensum	*weigh*
perdō, perdere, perdidī, perditum	*lose*
pergō, pergere, perrexī, perrectum	*continue*
permittō, permittere, permīsī, permissum	*allow*
petō, petere, petīvī, petītum	*seek*
pōnō, pōnere, posuī, positum	*put*
praedīcō, praedīcere, praedixī, praedictum	*predict*
premō, premere, pressī, pressum	*press*
prōcēdō, prōcēdere, prōcessī, prōcessum	*advance*
prōdō, prōdere, prōdidī, prōditum	*give forth*
prōmittō, prōmittere, prōmīsī, prōmissum	*promise*
prōpōnō, prōpōnere, prōposuī, prōpositum	*propose*
quaerō, quaerere, quaesīvī, quaesītum	*seek*
quiescō, quiescere, quiēvī, quiētum	*rest*
rapiō, rapere, rapuī, raptum	*snatch*
recēdō, recēdere, recessī, recessum	*withdraw*
reddō, reddere, reddidī, redditum	*return*
regō, regere, rexī, rectum	*rule*
relinquō, relinquere, relīquī, relictum	*leave*
requīrō, requīrere, requīsīvī, requīsītum	*seek*
revertō, revertere, revertī, reversum	*turn back*
rumpō, rumpere, rūpī, ruptum	*break*
scrībō, scrībere, scripsī, scriptum	*write*
solvō, solvere, solvī, solūtum	*loosen*
spargō, spargere, sparsī, sparsum	*sprinkle*
sternō, sternere, strāvī, strātum	*strew*
sūmō, sūmere, sumpsī, sumptum	*take up*
surgō, surgere, surrexī, surrectum	*rise*
tangō, tangere, tetigī, tactum	*touch*
tendō, tendere, tetendī, tentum	*stretch*
trādō, trādere, trādidī, trāditum	*hand over*
trahō, trahere, traxī, tractum	*drag*
vehō, vehere, vexī, vectum	*carry*
vertō, vertere, vertī, versum	*turn*
vincō, vincere, vīcī, victum	*conquer*
vīvō, vīvere, vixī, victum	*live*

Third -iō conjugation verbs

accipiō, accipere, accēpī, acceptum	*receive*
aspiciō, aspicere, aspexī, aspectum	*look at*
capiō, capere, cēpī, captum	*take*
conficiō, conficere, confēcī, confectum	*construct*

conspiciō, conspicere, conspexī, conspectum	*catch sight of*
cupiō, cupere, cupīvī, cupītum	*desire*
dēcipiō, dēcipere, dēcēpī, dēceptum	*deceive*
dēficiō, dēficere, dēfēcī, dēfectum	*lack, fail*
efficiō, efficere, effēcī, effectum	*cause*
ēripiō, ēripere, ēripuī, ēreptum	*snatch away*
excipiō, excipere, excēpī, exceptum	*receive*
faciō, facere, fēcī, factum	*make, do*
fugiō, fugere, fūgī	*flee*
iaciō, iacere, iēcī, iactum	*throw*
incipiō, incipere, incēpī, inceptum	*begin*
interficiō, interficere, interfēcī, interfectum	*kill*
pariō, parere, peperī, partum	*give birth*
percutiō, percutere, percussī, percussum	*strike*
perficiō, perficere, perfēcī, perfectum	*complete*
praecipiō, praecipere, praecēpī, praeceptum	*teach*
recipiō, recipere, recēpī, receptum	*receive*
respiciō, respicere, respexī, respectum	*look back*
suscipiō, suscipere, suscēpī, susceptum	*take up*

Nouns • Case endings • First-declension nouns

Noun characteristics and case endings

Like Latin verbs, whose characteristics are marked by endings, Latin nouns have case endings to express the following characteristics:

1. *Case*, which indicates the function of the word in the sentence
2. *Number*, which indicates whether the word is singular or plural
3. *Gender*, which indicates the arbitrary grammatical gender of the word

Latin compresses all three of these characteristics into a single case ending. If you can recognize the case ending, you can quickly and easily decode the case and number of a noun. Because gender is somewhat arbitrary, however, the ending doesn't always reveal a noun's gender.

Case functions

There are six cases in Latin.

CASE NAME	ABBREVIATION	MOST COMMON FUNCTION IN A SENTENCE
NOMINATIVE	nom.	Subject of the verb
GENITIVE	gen.	Possessor of another noun
DATIVE	dat.	Indirect object of the verb
ACCUSATIVE	acc.	Direct object of the verb
ABLATIVE	abl.	Adverbial use
VOCATIVE	voc.	Direct address

Indicate which case the italicized word(s) in each of the following sentences would use in Latin.

1. *Quintus* is acting strangely. _____

2. No one has seen *Flavia* in a while. _____

3. We found *Quintus and Flavia* out in the street. _____

4. A friend offered *Flavia* some help. _____

5. *Quintus* is not very charitable toward his neighbors. _____

6. *Quintus*, when will you give me my money? _____

7. *Quintus's* tools were left out in the rain. _____

8. *Flavia* saw some beautiful birds through her window. _____

9. The intruder was captured *by Flavia*. _____

10. Let's all give *Quintus and Flavia* a round of applause. _____

Declensions

Another important piece of information about a noun is its declension. Latin has five declensions, each with its own set of case endings. Every noun in Latin (except irregular nouns) follows one of these five patterns of case endings. In order to decode the case, number, and gender of a noun, you need to know which declension it belongs to.

The first declension

The pattern of case endings for the first declension is built around the sound -**a**-. Most first-declension nouns—but not all—are feminine in gender. All first-declension nouns do, however, have a genitive singular form that ends in -**ae**. Here are the endings of first-declension nouns:

NUMBER	CASE	ENDING
SINGULAR	NOMINATIVE	-a
	GENITIVE	-ae
	DATIVE	-ae
	ACCUSATIVE	-am
	ABLATIVE	-ā
	VOCATIVE	-a
PLURAL	NOMINATIVE	-ae
	GENITIVE	-ārum
	DATIVE	-īs
	ACCUSATIVE	-ās
	ABLATIVE	-īs
	VOCATIVE	-ae

To find the stem of any noun, drop the genitive ending of the second part of the dictionary entry; what's left is the stem. For example:

DICTIONARY ENTRY		NOUN STEM
lacrima, lacrimae *f.* tear		lacrim**ae**

NUMBER	CASE	ENDING
SINGULAR	NOMINATIVE	lacrim**a**
	GENITIVE	lacrim**ae**
	DATIVE	lacrim**ae**
	ACCUSATIVE	lacrim**am**
	ABLATIVE	lacrim**ā**
	VOCATIVE	lacrim**a**
PLURAL	NOMINATIVE	lacrim**ae**
	GENITIVE	lacrim**ārum**
	DATIVE	lacrim**īs**
	ACCUSATIVE	lacrim**ās**
	ABLATIVE	lacrim**īs**
	VOCATIVE	lacrim**ae**

EXERCISE 4·2

Give the stem of each of the following nouns.

1. via _____

2. turba _____

3. historia _____

4. amīcitia _____

5. fābula _____

6. pugna _____

7. glōria _____

8. aura _____

9. poēta _____

10. māteria _____

The nominative and accusative cases

The most important cases are the nominative and the accusative, because these two cases indicate functions that are found in nearly every sentence: the subject of the verb and the direct object of the verb. (Notice that the case ending is all the information you need to understand the relationships and functions of the words in a sentence; the order of the words does not give you this information.)

Give the correct nominative or accusative form of each of the following nouns.

1. mora (*nom. sg.*) _____

2. culpa (*acc. pl.*) _____

3. patria (*acc. sg.*) _____

4. silva (*nom. pl.*) _____

5. coma (*acc. sg.*) _____

6. rosa (*acc. pl.*) _____

7. littera (*nom. pl.*) _____

8. victōria (*acc. pl.*) _____

9. scientia (*nom. sg.*) _____

10. herba (*nom. pl.*) _____

Keeping the same case, transform each of the following nouns into its opposite number, singular to plural or plural to singular. Some nouns may have more than one opposite-number form.

1. Mūsam _____

2. fugās _____

3. cūra _____

4. stellae _____

5. portam _____

6. rīpae _____

7. memoriam _____

8. fēminās _____

9. aqua _____

10. fāmae _____

Now that we have studied subjects, verbs, and objects, we can explore how cases and verb forms interact in Latin sentences. Notice how the case ending of each noun in the following sentences indicates its function, and how the personal ending of each verb indicates its person and number.

Quint**us** aqu**am** bib**it**.	*Quintus is drinking the water.*
Histori**am** scrīb**ō**.	*I am writing history.*
Puell**ae** silv**am** intra**nt**.	*The girls are entering the forest.*

Translate each of the following sentences into English.

1. Mūsās semper poētae amant. _____

2. Fugit īram. _____

3. Trōia iam stat. _____

4. Conficis viam? _____

5. Dēfendō vītam. _____

6. Petimus amīcitiās. _____

7. Nōn laudātis comam. _____

8. Domina saepe imperat. _____

9. Nātūra tandem quiescit. _____

10. Nunc vident stellās. _____

VOCABULARY

Common first-declension nouns

amīcitia, amīcitiae (*f.*)	*friendship*	historia, historiae (*f.*)	*history*
anima, animae (*f.*)	*soul*	hōra, hōrae (*f.*)	*hour*
aqua, aquae (*f.*)	*water*	īra, īrae (*f.*)	*anger*
aura, aurae (*f.*)	*breeze*	Italia, Italiae (*f.*)	*Italy*
causa, causae (*f.*)	*cause*	lacrima, lacrimae (*f.*)	*tear*
coma, comae (*f.*)	*hair*	lingua, linguae (*f.*)	*language*
cōpia, cōpiae (*f.*)	*abundance*	littera, litterae (*f.*)	*letter*
culpa, culpae (*f.*)	*fault*	lūna, lūnae (*f.*)	*moon*
cūra, cūrae (*f.*)	*concern*	māteria, māteriae (*f.*)	*stuff*
custōdia, custōdiae (*f.*)	*protection*	memoria, memoriae (*f.*)	*memory*
dea, deae (*f.*)	*goddess*	mensa, mensae (*f.*)	*table*
dīvitiae, dīvitiārum (*f.pl.*)	*wealth*	mora, morae (*f.*)	*delay*
domina, dominae (*f.*)	*mistress*	Mūsa, Mūsae (*f.*)	*Muse*
fābula, fābulae (*f.*)	*story*	nātūra, nātūrae (*f.*)	*nature*
fāma, fāmae (*f.*)	*reputation*	patria, patriae (*f.*)	*country*
fēmina, fēminae (*f.*)	*woman*	pecūnia, pecūniae (*f.*)	*money*
fīlia, fīliae (*f.*)	*daughter*	poena, poenae (*f.*)	*penalty*
flamma, flammae (*f.*)	*flame*	poēta, poētae (*m.*)	*poet*
forma, formae (*f.*)	*beauty*	porta, portae (*f.*)	*gate*
fortūna, fortūnae (*f.*)	*fortune*	puella, puellae (*f.*)	*girl*
fuga, fugae (*f.*)	*fleeing*	pugna, pugnae (*f.*)	*fight*
Gallia, Galliae (*f.*)	*Gaul*	rīpa, rīpae (*f.*)	*bank*
glōria, glōriae (*f.*)	*glory*	Rōma, Rōmae (*f.*)	*Rome*
grātia, grātiae (*f.*)	*charm*	rosa, rosae (*f.*)	*rose*
herba, herbae (*f.*)	*grass*	sapientia, sapientiae (*f.*)	*wisdom*

scientia, scientiae (*f.*)	*knowledge*	turba, turbae (*f.*)	*uproar*
sententia, sententiae (*f.*)	*thought*	umbra, umbrae (*f.*)	*shade*
silva, silvae (*f.*)	*forest*	unda, undae (*f.*)	*wave*
stella, stellae (*f.*)	*star*	via, viae (*f.*)	*street*
tenebrae, tenebrārum (*f.pl.*)	*shadows*	victōria, victōriae (*f.*)	*victory*
terra, terrae (*f.*)	*land*	vīta, vītae (*f.*)	*life*
Trōia, Trōiae (*f.*)	*Troy*		

More case endings: genitive, dative, ablative, and vocative

The remaining four cases perform functions in a sentence that are less essential than subject or object, but still important for understanding the sentence.

The genitive case ending marks a word that has possession of another noun.

cūrae **Flāviae**	*Flavia's concerns*
portam **Rōmae**	*the gate of Rome*

The dative case ending marks a noun that is indirectly affected by the action of the verb; the noun is often called an *indirect object*.

Aquam **puellae** dat.	*He is giving water to the girl.*
Mūsae respondet.	*He answers to the Muse.*

The ablative case ending marks a variety of adverbial relationships to the verb. An ablative noun is also often the object of a preposition.

Formā dēcipit.	*He deceives with his beauty.*
Pecūniam in **rīpā** vidēs.	*You see the money on the bank.*

The vocative case ending marks direct address to a person or thing. It is the least common case ending.

Ō **lūna**, quō errās?	*O moon, where are you straying to?*

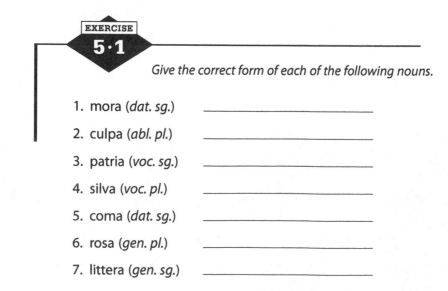

EXERCISE 5·1

Give the correct form of each of the following nouns.

1. mora (*dat. sg.*) _____
2. culpa (*abl. pl.*) _____
3. patria (*voc. sg.*) _____
4. silva (*voc. pl.*) _____
5. coma (*dat. sg.*) _____
6. rosa (*gen. pl.*) _____
7. littera (*gen. sg.*) _____

8. victōria (*abl. pl.*) _____

9. scientia (*dat. sg.*) _____

10. herba (*abl. pl.*) _____

EXERCISE
5·2

List all possible cases for each of the following nouns.

1. pecūniae _____

2. terrīs _____

3. animā _____

4. fīliam _____

5. causīs _____

6. fortūnae _____

7. custōdiārum _____

8. dominās _____

9. sapientiā _____

10. Trōiam _____

EXERCISE
5·3

Keeping the same case, transform each of the following nouns into its opposite number, singular to plural or plural to singular. Some nouns may have more than one opposite-number form.

1. Mūsae _____ 6. rīpīs _____

2. fugīs _____ 7. memoriae _____

3. cūrā _____ 8. fēminīs _____

4. stellārum _____ 9. aquae _____

5. porta _____ 10. fāmam _____

Give the correct Latin form of each of the following English nouns.

1. life (*dat. pl.*) _____

2. anger (*gen. pl.*) _____

3. girl (*acc. sg.*) _____

4. table (*abl. sg.*) _____

5. abundance (*acc. pl.*) _____

6. thought (*gen. pl.*) _____

7. nature (*nom. sg.*) _____

8. goddess (*gen. sg.*) _____

9. charm (*dat. pl.*) _____

10. moon (*abl. sg.*) _____

Translate each of the following sentences into English.

1. Fābulās fēminae dīcit.

_____

2. Ornant rosīs mensam.

_____

3. Scientia dat memoriae sapientiam.

_____

4. Ō Italia, haud ēvādis culpam!

_____

5. Sub umbrā silvārum dormiō.

_____

6. Comam lacrimīs spargit.

_____

7. Īra deārum facit cūrās.

_____

8. Fīliās praebēmus patriae.

_____

9. Post victōriam rapiunt pecūniam Trōiae.

_____

10. Linguā narrātis.

_____

Personal pronouns

A pronoun is used to refer to another noun. Personal pronouns are a special sub-category of pronouns that refer to the people involved in an action: *I*, *you*, *him*, and so on. We have already seen that Latin does not always need to use a noun or pronoun to indicate who is performing the action of a verb, because the ending of the verb contains that information itself. But Latin frequently uses personal pronouns in cases other than the nominative.

CASE	FIRST PERSON		SECOND PERSON	
	I	*we*	*you*	*you all*
NOMINATIVE	ego	nōs	tū	vōs
GENITIVE	meī	nostrī	tuī	vestrī
DATIVE	mihi	nōbīs	tibi	vōbīs
ACCUSATIVE	mē	nōs	tē	vōs
ABLATIVE	mē	nōbīs	tē	vōbīs

There is no specific personal pronoun in Latin for the third person. Latin either uses a specific noun, omits the noun and lets the verb's ending show the subject, or uses a demonstrative pronoun like **is ea id**.

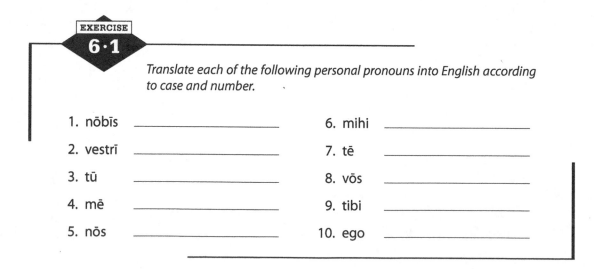

EXERCISE
6·1

Translate each of the following personal pronouns into English according to case and number.

1. nōbīs _____

2. vestrī _____

3. tū _____

4. mē _____

5. nōs _____

6. mihi _____

7. tē _____

8. vōs _____

9. tibi _____

10. ego _____

EXERCISE 6·2

Give the Latin personal pronoun that would be used for the italicized word(s) in each of the following sentences.

1. Did you see *us* yesterday? _____

2. I know it is very important *to you* (*sg.*). _____

3. *You* (*sg.*) never showed us that! _____

4. You never showed *us* that! _____

5. Here's what *I* think. _____

6. I neglected *you* (*pl.*), and I'm sorry. _____

7. His voice charmed *me*. _____

8. Would you like to come with *us*? _____

9. The traitor handed *you* (*sg.*) over to the enemy. _____

10. They gave *me* enough food for the next week. _____

EXERCISE 6·3

Translate each of the following sentences into English.

1. Tibi nōn noceō. _____

2. Nōs pōnis in flammīs. _____

3. Quid dē mē existimātis? _____

4. Memoria vestrī iterum vīvit. _____

5. Fāma Rōmae nōbīs placet. _____

6. Ego tamen causam habeō. _____

7. Terra mē sustinet. _____

8. Ā tē nunc petō moram. _____

9. Nōs lūnam paene tangimus. _____

10. Tū metuis poenam. _____

·7· ◆ Second-declension nouns

The second declension functions exactly like the first declension, but uses a different set of case endings to indicate the noun's function in a sentence. This declension is built around the sound -o-. The case ending attaches to the stem of the noun. Most, but not all, second-declension nouns are masculine or neuter. All second-declension nouns have a genitive singular form that ends in -ī. Here are the endings of second-declension nouns:

NUMBER	CASE	MASCULINE ENDING	NEUTER ENDING
SINGULAR	NOMINATIVE	-us	-um
	GENITIVE	-ī	-ī
	DATIVE	-ō	-ō
	ACCUSATIVE	-um	-um
	ABLATIVE	-ō	-ō
	VOCATIVE	-e	-um
PLURAL	NOMINATIVE	-ī	-a
	GENITIVE	-ōrum	-ōrum
	DATIVE	-īs	-īs
	ACCUSATIVE	-ōs	-a
	ABLATIVE	-īs	-īs
	VOCATIVE	-ī	-a

Notice that neuter words have the same case endings for the nominative, accusative, and vocative cases, in both the singular and the plural. This pattern is consistent throughout Latin.

A few nouns in the second declension end in -r or -er. With the exception of the nominative and vocative singular, these nouns have the same forms as other second-declension nouns. On the next page is an example.

NUMBER	CASE	FORM
SINGULAR	NOMINATIVE	vir
	GENITIVE	vir**ī**
	DATIVE	vir**ō**
	ACCUSATIVE	vir**um**
	ABLATIVE	vir**ō**
	VOCATIVE	vir
PLURAL	NOMINATIVE	vir**ī**
	GENITIVE	vir**ōrum**
	DATIVE	vir**īs**
	ACCUSATIVE	vir**ōs**
	ABLATIVE	vir**īs**
	VOCATIVE	vir**ī**

EXERCISE 7·1

Give the stem of each of the following nouns.

1. puer _____
2. bellum _____
3. ōtium _____
4. thēsaurus _____
5. tergum _____

6. ager _____
7. nuntius _____
8. torus _____
9. humus _____
10. minister _____

EXERCISE 7·2

Give the correct form of each of the following nouns.

1. hortus (*acc. sg.*) _____
2. verbum (*nom. pl.*) _____
3. ingenium (*dat. pl.*) _____
4. vīnum (*gen. sg.*) _____
5. magister (*acc. sg.*) _____
6. rogus (*voc. pl.*) _____
7. animus (*dat. pl.*) _____
8. locus (*dat. sg.*) _____
9. praemium (*acc. pl.*) _____
10. pontus (*abl. sg.*) _____

List all possible cases for each of the following nouns.

1. servō _____

2. gladiīs _____

3. dominī _____

4. virīs _____

5. deum _____

6. nāte _____

7. membra _____

8. digitus _____

9. argentī _____

10. agrum _____

Keeping the same case, transform each of the following noun forms into its opposite number, singular to plural or plural to singular. Some nouns may have more than one opposite-number form.

1. somnum _____

2. amīcō _____

3. oculī _____

4. vōtī _____

5. librōs _____

6. gaudiīs _____

7. Phoebum _____

8. templa _____

9. numerō _____

10. puerīs _____

Give the correct Latin form of each of the following nouns.

1. fault (gen. pl.) _____

2. horse (acc. pl.) _____

3. empire (nom. pl.) _____

4. attendant (gen. sg.) _____

5. husband (*nom. sg.*) _____

6. camp (*gen. pl.*) _____

7. weapon (*abl. pl.*) _____

8. duty (*dat. sg.*) _____

9. son (*acc. sg.*) _____

10. slave (*acc. pl.*) _____

EXERCISE

7·6

Translate each of the following sentences into English.

1. Servī agrōs colunt.

_____

2. Pretium gladiī ignōrātis.

_____

3. Augustum triumphō celebrant.

_____

4. In terrā et caelō deōs nōn cernis.

_____

5. Populus consilium vestrī contemnat.

_____

6. Iuga in hortīs impōnō.

_____

7. Tunc fēmina cibum capit.

_____

8. Principium convīviī signō postulant.

_____

9. Arma iuxtā mūrōs āmittis?

_____

10. Sī vīnum bibis, gaudium habēs.

_____

Common second-declension nouns

aevum, aevī (n.)	age	minister, ministrī (m.)	attendant
ager, agrī (m.)	field	modus, modī (m.)	manner
amīcus, amīcī (m.)	friend	mundus, mundī (m.)	world
animus, animī (m.)	mind	mūrus, mūrī (m.)	wall
annus, annī (m.)	year	nātus, nātī (m.)	child
argentum, argentī (n.)	silver	negōtium, negōtiī (n.)	business
arma, armōrum (n.pl.)	weapons	numerus, numerī (m.)	number
arvum, arvī (n.)	field	nuntius, nuntiī (m.)	messenger
astrum, astrī (n.)	star	oculus, oculī (m.)	eye
Augustus, Augustī (m.)	Augustus	officium, officiī (n.)	duty
aurum, aurī (n.)	gold	ōtium, ōtiī (n.)	leisure
auxilium, auxiliī (n.)	help	pelagus, pelagī (n.)	sea
Bacchus, Bacchī (m.)	Bacchus	perīculum, perīculī (n.)	danger
bellum, bellī (n.)	war	Phoebus, Phoebī (m.)	Phoebus
caelum, caelī (n.)	sky	pontus, pontī (m.)	sea
campus, campī (m.)	plain	populus, populī (m.)	people
castra, castrōrum (n.pl.)	camp	praemium, praemiī (n.)	reward
chorus, chorī (m.)	chorus	pretium, pretiī (n.)	price
cibus, cibī (m.)	food	principium, principiī (n.)	beginning
consilium, consiliī (n.)	plan	proelium, proeliī (n.)	battle
convīvium, convīviī (n.)	party	puer, puerī (m.)	boy
damnum, damnī (n.)	loss	regnum, regnī (n.)	kingdom
deus, deī (m.)	god	rogus, rogī (m.)	pyre
digitus, digitī (m.)	finger	saeculum, saeculī (n.)	age
dominus, dominī (m.)	master	saxum, saxī (n.)	rock
dōnum, dōnī (n.)	gift	sepulcrum, sepulcrī (n.)	tomb
equus, equī (m.)	horse	servus, servī (m.)	slave
exemplum, exemplī (n.)	example	signum, signī (n.)	sign
famulus, famulī (m.)	slave	silentium, silentiī (n.)	silence
fātum, fātī (n.)	fate	somnus, somnī (m.)	sleep
ferrum, ferrī (n.)	iron	spatium, spatiī (n.)	space
fīlius, fīliī (m.)	son	studium, studiī (n.)	enthusiasm
Gallus, Gallī (m.)	a Gaul	tectum, tectī (n.)	roof
gaudium, gaudiī (n.)	joy	tēlum, tēlī (n.)	spear
gladius, gladiī (m.)	sword	templum, templī (n.)	temple
hortus, hortī (m.)	garden	tergum, tergī (n.)	back
humus, humī (f.)	ground	thēsaurus, thēsaurī (m.)	treasure
imperium, imperiī (n.)	empire	torus, torī (m.)	couch
ingenium, ingeniī (n.)	talent	triumphus, triumphī (m.)	triumph
iūdicium, iūdiciī (n.)	trial	ventus, ventī (m.)	wind
iugum, iugī (n.)	yoke	verbum, verbī (n.)	word
liber, librī (m.)	book	vinculum, vinculī (n.)	chain
locus, locī (m.)	place	vīnum, vīnī (n.)	wine
magister, magistrī (m.)	teacher	vir, virī (m.)	man
marītus, marītī (m.)	husband	vitium, vitiī (n.)	fault
membrum, membrī (n.)	limb	vōtum, vōtī (n.)	vow

Noun and adjective agreement • Adjectives ending in -us -a -um

Adjectives describe nouns. In Latin, you can tell which adjective describes which noun only by their agreement. Agreement means that in order to describe a noun, an adjective must have the same case, number, and gender as the noun. Sometimes, the case endings of both words look the same, but often the case endings look different.

There are two main types of adjectives, each with its own pattern of endings. Fortunately, the endings of the first type are similar to those of the noun declensions you already know; this type is referred to as *first/second-declension adjectives*, or the **-us -a -um** type. The case endings of these adjectives are identical to the endings of first- and second-declension nouns combined. Here are the endings of **-us -a -um** adjectives:

NUMBER	CASE	MASCULINE	FEMININE	NEUTER
SINGULAR	NOMINATIVE	-us	-a	-um
	GENITIVE	-ī	-ae	-ī
	DATIVE	-ō	-ae	-ō
	ACCUSATIVE	-um	-am	-um
	ABLATIVE	-ō	-ā	-ō
	VOCATIVE	-e	-a	-um
PLURAL	NOMINATIVE	-ī	-ae	-a
	GENITIVE	-ōrum	-ārum	-ōrum
	DATIVE	-īs	-īs	-īs
	ACCUSATIVE	-ōs	-ās	-a
	ABLATIVE	-īs	-īs	-īs
	VOCATIVE	-ī	-ae	-a

There is also a small set of adjectives that end in **-r -ra -rum**. The stem for these is the same as that of second-declension nouns in **-r** or **-er**.

A few **-us -a -um** adjectives have different forms for the genitive and dative singular. Included in this group are **ūnus, nullus, ullus, sōlus, alius, tōtus,** and **alter**. Here is an example of this pattern:

NUMBER	CASE	MASCULINE	FEMININE	NEUTER
SINGULAR	NOMINATIVE	tōtus	tōta	tōtum
	GENITIVE	tōt**īus**	tōt**īus**	tōt**īus**
	DATIVE	tōt**ī**	tōt**ī**	tōt**ī**
	ACCUSATIVE	tōtum	tōtam	tōtum
	ABLATIVE	tōtō	tōtā	tōtō
	VOCATIVE	tōte	tōta	tōtum
PLURAL	NOMINATIVE	tōtī	tōtae	tōta
	GENITIVE	tōtōrum	tōtārum	tōtōrum
	DATIVE	tōtīs	tōtīs	tōtīs
	ACCUSATIVE	tōtōs	tōtās	tōta
	ABLATIVE	tōtīs	tōtīs	tōtīs
	VOCATIVE	tōtī	tōtae	tōta

EXERCISE 8·1

Give the form of the adjective in parentheses that agrees with each of the following nouns.

1. (prīmus -a -um) proelium _____

2. (novus -a -um) mūrōrum _____

3. (adversus -a -um) undā _____

4. (nōtus -a -um) exemplī _____

5. (saevus -a -um) linguae _____

6. (maestus -a -um) poenam _____

7. (optimus -a -um) tectīs _____

8. (tener tenera tenerum) populōs _____

9. (mīrus -a -um) sepulcra _____

10. (tardus -a -um) hōrae _____

EXERCISE 8·2

Keeping the same case, transform each of the following adjective-noun phrases into its opposite number, singular to plural or plural to singular. Some phrases may have more than one opposite-number form.

1. superbōrum saeculōrum _____

2. beātum annum _____

3. aequum pretium _____

4. aeternam umbram _____

5. albī saxī _____

6. dīversīs fātīs _____

7. dīvārum deārum _____

8. pūrae flammae _____

9. citō ferrō _____

10. cārī ōtiī _____

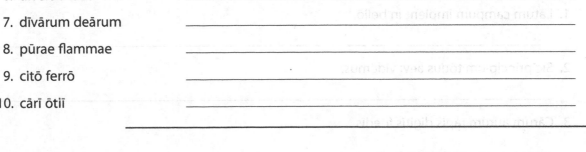

EXERCISE 8·3

From the following adjective-noun phrases, choose those in which the adjectives agree properly with their nouns.

immensō deō	placida bellī	mortuus consilium	singulās fēminās
piōs ventus	dūrīs regnīs	optimōrum poētārum	vīcīna terra
nūdō thēsaurum	ūniversīs auxiliīs	bonā fortūnā	perpetuae pugnārum
paucum damnum	candida bellō	malō caelō	ultimī perīcula
fessīs magistrīs	falsō studiīs	dīvīnārum scientiārum	vīvus Gallus

EXERCISE 8·4

Translate each of the following adjective-noun phrases into Latin.

1. wandering breeze (*nom. pl.*) _____

2. miserable year (*dat. pl.*) _____

3. worthy soul (*acc. pl.*) _____

4. pleasant Bacchus (*voc. sg.*) _____

5. beautiful world (*abl. sg.*) _____

6. ancient trial (*nom. pl.*) _____

7. unknown gift (*abl. pl.*) _____

8. large number (*acc. sg.*) _____

9. doubtful silence (*nom. sg.*) _____

10. royal business (*gen. pl.*) _____

Translate each of the following sentences into English.

1. Lātum campum implent in bellō.

_____

2. Sīc principium tōtīus aevī vidēmus.

_____

3. Cārum aurum rapis digitīs foedīs.

_____

4. Consiliō certō templī portās inveniunt.

_____

5. Arvum sacrum prō tē teneō.

_____

6. Dē mūrīs altīs descendimus.

_____

7. Fīliō integrō et dīvīnō vōta dant.

_____

8. Dīvitiae etiam officium publicum saepe superant.

_____

9. Ideō litterās multās tibi mittō.

_____

10. Proelia saeva vōs suscipitis.

_____

VOCABULARY

Common adjectives ending in -us -a -um

adversus adversa adversum	*adverse*	beātus beāta beātum	*blessed*
aeger aegra aegrum	*sick*	blandus blanda blandum	*charming*
aequus aequa aequum	*equal*	bonus bona bonum	*good*
aeternus aeterna aeternum	*eternal*	caecus caeca caecum	*blind*
albus alba album	*white*	candidus candida candidum	*bright*
aliēnus aliēna aliēnum	*another's*	cārus cāra cārum	*dear*
altus alta altum	*high*	castus casta castum	*pure*
antīquus antīqua antīquum	*ancient*	certus certa certum	*sure*
aptus apta aptum	*fitting*	cēterus cētera cēterum	*other*
aureus aurea aureum	*golden*	citus cita citum	*quick*

clārus clāra clārum	famous
cunctus cuncta cunctum	all together
densus densa densum	thick
dexter dextera dexterum	right
dignus digna dignum	worthy
dīversus dīversa dīversum	different
dīvīnus dīvīna dīvīnum	divine
dīvus dīva dīvum	divine
dubius dubia dubium	doubtful
dūrus dūra dūrum	hard
extrēmus extrēma extrēmum	farthest
falsus falsa falsum	deceptive
ferus fera ferum	wild
fessus fessa fessum	tired
festus festa festum	holiday
foedus foeda foedum	foul
Graecus Graeca Graecum	Greek
grātus grāta grātum	thankful
hūmānus hūmāna hūmānum	civilized
ignōtus ignōta ignōtum	unknown
immensus immensa immensum	immeasurable
improbus improba improbum	wicked
inferus infera inferum	lowest
inimīcus inimīca inimīcum	hostile
integer integra integrum	intact
iūcundus iūcunda iūcundum	pleasant
iustus iusta iustum	fair
laetus laeta laetum	cheerful
Latīnus Latīna Latīnum	Latin
lātus lāta lātum	wide
līber lībera līberum	free
longus longa longum	long
maestus maesta maestum	sad
magnus magna magnum	large
malus mala malum	bad
medius media medium	middle
mīrus mīra mīrum	wonderful
miser misera miserum	miserable
mortuus mortua mortuum	dead
multus multa multum	many
mundus munda mundum	clean
necessārius necessāria necessārium	necessary
niger nigra nigrum	black
nocturnus nocturna nocturnum	nighttime
noster nostra nostrum	our
nōtus nōta nōtum	famous
novus nova novum	new
nūdus nūda nūdum	naked

nullus nulla nullum	none
obvius obvia obvium	in the way
parvus parva parvum	small
paucus pauca paucum	few
paulus paula paulum	small
perpetuus perpetua perpetuum	continuous
pius pia pium	dutiful
placidus placida placidum	calm
plēnus plēna plēnum	full
praecipuus praecipua praecipuum	special
proprius propria proprium	own
proximus proxima proximum	closest
publicus publica publicum	public
pulcher pulchra pulchrum	beautiful
pūrus pūra pūrum	pure
quantus quanta quantum	how great
rārus rāra rārum	uncommon
rectus recta rectum	correct
rēgius rēgia rēgium	royal
reliquus reliqua reliquum	remaining
Rōmānus Rōmāna Rōmānum	Roman
rusticus rustica rusticum	country
sacer sacra sacrum	sacred
saevus saeva saevum	cruel
sanctus sancta sanctum	sacred
sēcūrus sēcūra sēcūrum	carefree
singulus singula singulum	one each
socius socia socium	companion
sollicitus sollicita sollicitum	worried
sōlus sōla sōlum	only
superbus superba superbum	haughty
tantus tanta tantum	so great
tardus tarda tardum	slow
tener tenera tenerum	tender
tōtus tōta tōtum	whole
tūtus tūta tūtum	safe
ullus ulla ullum	any
ūniversus ūniversa ūniversum	all together
vacuus vacua vacuum	empty
vagus vaga vagum	wandering
varius varia varium	varied
vērus vēra vērum	true
vīcīnus vīcīna vīcīnum	neighboring
vīvus vīva vīvum	alive

◆9◆ The present tense of sum • Predicate sentences

The present tense of sum

The most common verb in Latin, as in most languages, is the verb that means *to be*. In Latin, it is an irregular verb, but it uses the same personal endings you already know. Here is the present tense of **sum**:

	SINGULAR		PLURAL	
FIRST PERSON	sum	*I am*	sumus	*we are*
SECOND PERSON	es	*you are*	estis	*you are*
THIRD PERSON	est	*he/she/it is*	sunt	*they are*

Predicate sentences

Sometimes all you want to say is that one thing equals something else. In this case, there is no action verb or direct object involved. Sentences like this are called *predicate sentences*, and they use a verb like **sum**. You can think of the verb **sum** as an equals sign, and the two people or things being equated are both in the nominative case.

Italia est patria mea.   *Italy is my country.*
Nōs sumus puellae.   *We are girls.*

Predicate nominatives, predicate adjectives, and agreement

If a predicate sentence is equating two nouns, one is the subject and the other is a predicate nominative. If the sentence is equating a noun with an adjective, the noun is the subject and the adjective is a predicate adjective. Predicate nominatives only have to agree with the subject in case. Predicate adjectives, though, like all other adjectives, have to agree with the subject in case, number, and gender.

Tenebrae sunt nigrae.   *The shadows are black.*
Somnus est blandus.   *Sleep is charming.*

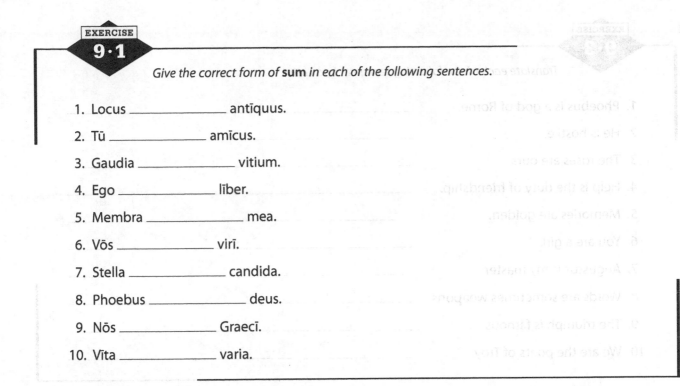

Give the correct form of sum in each of the following sentences.

1. Locus _____ antīquus.

2. Tū _____ amīcus.

3. Gaudia _____ vitium.

4. Ego _____ līber.

5. Membra _____ mea.

6. Vōs _____ virī.

7. Stella _____ candida.

8. Phoebus _____ deus.

9. Nōs _____ Graecī.

10. Vīta _____ varia.

In each of the following sentences, give the correct form of the word in parentheses so that it agrees with the subject.

1. Praemium tuum est (equus) _____.

2. Deī Rōmānī sunt (maximus) _____.

3. Verbum est (causa) _____.

4. Nōs (*m.*) sumus (vērus) _____.

5. Poena est (vinculum) _____.

6. Pecūnia est (aliēnus) _____.

7. Virī sunt (dubius) _____.

8. Trōia est (regnum) _____.

9. Tū (*m.*) es (rusticus) _____.

10. Sepulcra sunt (Latīnus) _____.

Translate each of the following sentences into Latin.

1. Phoebus is a god of Rome. _____

2. He is hostile. _____

3. The roses are ours. _____

4. Help is the duty of friendship. _____

5. Memories are golden. _____

6. You are a girl. _____

7. Augustus is my master. _____

8. Words are sometimes weapons. _____

9. The triumph is famous. _____

10. We are the poets of Troy. _____

Translate each of the following sentences into English. Some are predicate sentences, and some are not.

1. Templum Graecum est sacrum. _____

2. Ventī in pelagō sunt placidī. _____

3. Equus caecus tibi mē reddit. _____

4. Sententia est mihi nōta. _____

5. Liber in castrīs Gallōrum est. _____

6. Vōs estis improbae sīcut servī. _____

7. Es dominus? _____

8. Tibi damus novum tectum. _____

9. Sum līber, nec famulus. _____

10. Fugae sunt plēnae perīculōrum. _____

Common irregular verbs

abeō, abīre, abiī, abitum	*go away*
absum, abesse, āfuī	*be away*
adeō, adīre, adiī, aditum	*approach*
adsum, adesse, adfuī	*be present*
afferō, afferre, attulī, allātum	*bring to*
āiō	*say*
auferō, auferre, abstulī, ablātum	*carry away*
coepī, coepisse, coeptum	*begin*
conferō, conferre, contulī, collātum	*bring together*
dēferō, dēferre, dētulī, dēlātum	*bring down*
dēsum, dēesse, dēfuī	*be lacking*
dō, dare, dedī, datum	*give*
edō, esse, ēdī, ēsum	*eat*
eō, īre, iī/īvī, itum	*go*
exeō, exīre, exīvī, exitum	*go out*
ferō, ferre, tulī, lātum	*bring, bear*
fīō, fīerī	*be made, become*
inferō, inferre, intulī, illātum	*bring in*
inquam	*say*
mālō, malle, māluī	*prefer*
meminī, meminisse	*remember*
nōlō, nolle, nōluī	*not want*
pereō, perīre, periī, peritum	*die*
possum, posse, potuī	*be able, can*
praetereō, praeterīre, praeteriī, praeteritum	*pass by*
prōsum, prōdesse, prōfuī	*benefit*
redeō, redīre, rediī, reditum	*return*
referō, referre, rettulī, relātum	*bring back, tell*
subeō, subīre, subiī, subitum	*go under*
sum, esse, fuī	*be*
supersum, superesse, superfuī	*outlive*
tollō, tollere, sustulī, sublātum	*lift, remove*
transeō, transīre, transīvī, transitum	*go across*
volō, velle, voluī	*want*

The imperfect tense

The imperfect tense expresses past time, but also—and this is important—a specific aspect of how actions occurred in past time. Imperfect verbs tell you that the action happened continually, or over a period of time, in the past. (This contrasts with an action that took a single moment or occurred instantaneously in the past; Latin uses the perfect tense for that action.) The usual English translation of the imperfect tense is *was _____ing*.

Quintus mē interrogābat.

Quintus was questioning me. /
Quintus used to question me.

Flāvia forēs claudēbat.

Flavia was closing the door. /
Flavia used to close the door.

EXERCISE
10·1

Indicate whether each of the following sentences would use the imperfect tense in Latin.

	Yes	No
1. The athlete fell during the race.	☐	☐
2. We used to have breakfast in that restaurant.	☐	☐
3. The whole time, nobody was listening to him.	☐	☐
4. We were all watching for the bus.	☐	☐
5. Someone broke all these eggs.	☐	☐
6. Did you take out the trash?	☐	☐
7. The room suddenly went dark.	☐	☐
8. I was hoping for a victory.	☐	☐
9. The fishermen caught lots of fish every day.	☐	☐
10. My fingers were stained with paint.	☐	☐

Marking the imperfect tense

To indicate that a verb is in the imperfect tense, Latin adds the tense marker **-bā-** between the present system root and the personal endings.

Present system root + **-bā-** + Active personal endings = Imperfect tense

Here are example charts of the imperfect tense for each conjugation:

First conjugation

amō, amāre, amāvī, amātum *love*
PRESENT SYSTEM ROOT   amā-

	SINGULAR		PLURAL	
FIRST PERSON	amā**bam**	*I was loving*	amā**bā**mus	*we were loving*
SECOND PERSON	amā**bās**	*you were loving*	amā**bā**tis	*you were loving*
THIRD PERSON	amā**bat**	*he/she/it was loving*	amā**bant**	*they were loving*

Second conjugation

teneō, tenēre, tenuī, tentum *hold*
PRESENT SYSTEM ROOT   tenē-

	SINGULAR		PLURAL	
FIRST PERSON	tenē**bam**	*I was holding*	tenē**bā**mus	*we were holding*
SECOND PERSON	tenē**bās**	*you were holding*	tenē**bā**tis	*you were holding*
THIRD PERSON	tenē**bat**	*he/she/it was holding*	tenē**bant**	*they were holding*

Third conjugation

pōnō, pōnere, posuī, positum *put*
PRESENT SYSTEM ROOT   pōne-

	SINGULAR		PLURAL	
FIRST PERSON	pōnē**bam**	*I was putting*	pōnē**bā**mus	*we were putting*
SECOND PERSON	pōnē**bās**	*you were putting*	pōnē**bā**tis	*you were putting*
THIRD PERSON	pōnē**bat**	*he/she/it was putting*	pōnē**bant**	*they were putting*

Third -iō conjugation

capiō, capere, cēpī, captum *take*
PRESENT SYSTEM ROOT   cape-

	SINGULAR		PLURAL	
FIRST PERSON	capiē**bam**	*I was taking*	capiē**bā**mus	*we were taking*
SECOND PERSON	capiē**bās**	*you were taking*	capiē**bā**tis	*you were taking*
THIRD PERSON	capiē**bat**	*he/she/it was taking*	capiē**bant**	*they were taking*

Fourth conjugation

audiō, audīre, audīvī, audītum *hear*
PRESENT SYSTEM ROOT   audī-

	SINGULAR		PLURAL	
FIRST PERSON	audiē**bam**	*I was hearing*	audiē**bā**mus	*we were hearing*
SECOND PERSON	audiē**bās**	*you were hearing*	audiē**bā**tis	*you were hearing*
THIRD PERSON	audiē**bat**	*he/she/it was hearing*	audiē**bant**	*they were hearing*

Note the slight changes in the third, third **-iō**, and fourth conjugations. In the third conjugation, the short root vowel strengthens to **-ē-**. In the third **-iō** and fourth conjugations, an **-ē-** appears between the root vowel and the tense marker.

10·2

Identify the person, number, and tense of each of the following verbs.

1. tacēbant _____
2. cessābam _____
3. accidit _____
4. cōgēbant _____
5. fundō _____
6. invidēbat _____
7. indicābās _____
8. labōrātis _____
9. intellegēbat _____
10. aspicimus _____

10·3

Give the correct form of each of the following verbs.

1. sedeō (*3 sg. imperfect*) _____
2. cantō (*3 pl. imperfect*) _____
3. comedō (*2 sg. imperfect*) _____
4. gerō (*3 sg. present*) _____
5. perdō (*1 pl. imperfect*) _____
6. sentiō (*2 pl. imperfect*) _____
7. cingō (*3 pl. present*) _____
8. neglegō (*2 sg. imperfect*) _____
9. sepeliō (*3 sg. imperfect*) _____
10. vigilō (*1 pl. imperfect*) _____

EXERCISE 10·4

Keeping the same person and number, transform each of the following present-tense verbs to the imperfect.

1. aperīmus _____
2. spērātis _____
3. ardēs _____
4. patent _____
5. scit _____

6. errāmus _____
7. monētis _____
8. veniō _____
9. appellant _____
10. laudat _____

EXERCISE 10·5

Translate each of the following verbs into English.

1. praebēbat _____
2. optābam _____
3. interficiunt _____
4. colēbās _____
5. nesciēbat _____

6. solētis _____
7. pugnābant _____
8. fīgēbāmus _____
9. parcēbat _____
10. augēbās _____

The future tense

The future tense expresses an action that will occur in the future. Like the present and imperfect tenses, the future is built from the present system root, a tense marker, and personal endings. The usual English translation is *will* _____.

Present system root + **-b-/-bi-/-bu-** or **-a-/-ē-** + Active personal endings
= Future tense

The first and second conjugations use the **-b-** markers for the future, but the third, third **-iō**, and fourth conjugations use **-ē-** as a tense marker. This distinction is important; otherwise, for example, it's difficult to tell a second-conjugation present tense from a third-conjugation future tense.

Here are example charts of the future tense for each conjugation:

First conjugation

amō, amāre, amāvī, amātum *love*
PRESENT SYSTEM ROOT amā-

	SINGULAR		PLURAL	
FIRST PERSON	amā**bō**	*I will love*	amā**bi**mus	*we will love*
SECOND PERSON	amā**bis**	*you will love*	amā**bi**tis	*you will love*
THIRD PERSON	amā**bit**	*he/she/it will love*	amā**bu**nt	*they will love*

Second conjugation

habeō, habēre, habuī, habitum *have*
PRESENT SYSTEM ROOT habē-

	SINGULAR		PLURAL	
FIRST PERSON	habē**bō**	*I will have*	habē**bi**mus	*we will have*
SECOND PERSON	habē**bis**	*you will have*	habē**bi**tis	*you will have*
THIRD PERSON	habē**bit**	*he/she/it will have*	habē**bu**nt	*they will have*

Third conjugation

agō, agere, ēgī, actum *drive, act*
PRESENT SYSTEM ROOT age-

	SINGULAR		PLURAL	
FIRST PERSON	ag**am**	*I will drive*	ag**ē**mus	*we will drive*
SECOND PERSON	ag**ē**s	*you will drive*	ag**ē**tis	*you will drive*
THIRD PERSON	ag**e**t	*he/she/it will drive*	ag**e**nt	*they will drive*

Third -iō conjugation

capiō, capere, cēpī, captum *take*
PRESENT SYSTEM ROOT   cape-

	SINGULAR		PLURAL	
FIRST PERSON	capiam	*I will take*	capiēmus	*we will take*
SECOND PERSON	capiēs	*you will take*	capiētis	*you will take*
THIRD PERSON	capiet	*he/she/it will take*	capient	*they will take*

Fourth conjugation

audiō, audīre, audīvī, audītum *hear*
PRESENT SYSTEM ROOT   audī-

	SINGULAR		PLURAL	
FIRST PERSON	audiam	*I will hear*	audiēmus	*we will hear*
SECOND PERSON	audiēs	*you will hear*	audiētis	*you will hear*
THIRD PERSON	audiet	*he/she/it will hear*	audient	*they will hear*

EXERCISE
11·1

Identify the person, number, and tense of each of the following verbs.

1. patēs   _____

2. cernēs   _____

3. pariēbat   _____

4. vacābit   _____

5. sternēmus   _____

6. discunt   _____

7. imperābant   _____

8. servient   _____

9. sciētis   _____

10. putābunt   _____

Give the correct form of each of the following verbs.

1. nōminō (*1 sg. future*) _____

2. cognoscō (*3 pl. future*) _____

3. iaciō (*2 sg. future*) _____

4. regnō (*3 sg. future*) _____

5. certō (*3 pl. imperfect*) _____

6. recipiō (*2 pl. future*) _____

7. sustineō (*3 sg. present*) _____

8. trahō (*2 sg. future*) _____

9. revertō (*3 sg. imperfect*) _____

10. addō (*1 pl. future*) _____

Keeping the same person and number, transform each of the following present-tense verbs to the future.

1. āmittit _____

2. tendō _____

3. bibimus _____

4. appāret _____

5. narrant _____

6. sonāmus _____

7. lūdunt _____

8. iungit _____

9. perveniunt _____

10. parātis _____

Translate each of the following verbs into English.

1. cupient _____

2. pendēbam _____

3. permittet _____

4. agitat _____

5. negābis _____

6. dormiam _____

7. induunt _____

8. merētis _____

9. portābunt _____

10. consulēmus _____

Translate each of the following verb phrases into Latin.

1. I will snatch _____

2. you (*sg.*) will press _____

3. he will care _____

4. we are touching _____

5. you (*pl.*) were believing _____

6. they will complete _____

7. she will advise _____

8. it used to deceive _____

9. they will train _____

10. we will save _____

The imperfect and future tenses of sum •
The irregular verb possum •
The present active infinitive

·12·

Sum

The verb **sum, esse, fuī** is irregular in the imperfect and future tenses.

Imperfect

	SINGULAR		PLURAL	
FIRST PERSON	eram	*I was*	erāmus	*we were*
SECOND PERSON	erās	*you were*	erātis	*you were*
THIRD PERSON	erat	*he/she/it was*	erant	*they were*

Future

	SINGULAR		PLURAL	
FIRST PERSON	erō	*I will be*	erimus	*we will be*
SECOND PERSON	eris	*you will be*	eritis	*you will be*
THIRD PERSON	erit	*he/she/it will be*	erunt	*they will be*

Possum

The irregular verb **possum, posse, potuī** *to be able* is a compound verb built from **potis** *able* and **sum** *to be*. To form the verb **possum**, the first part, from **potis**, generally shrinks to **pot-** or **pos-** and is then followed by the various forms of **sum**. If you know the forms of **sum**, it is easy to learn the forms of **possum**.

Present

	SINGULAR		PLURAL	
FIRST PERSON	possum	*I am able*	possumus	*we are able*
SECOND PERSON	potes	*you are able*	potestis	*you are able*
THIRD PERSON	potest	*he/she/it is able*	possunt	*they are able*

Imperfect

	SINGULAR		PLURAL	
FIRST PERSON	poteram	*I was able*	poterāmus	*we were able*
SECOND PERSON	poterās	*you were able*	poterātis	*you were able*
THIRD PERSON	poterat	*he/she/it was able*	poterant	*they were able*

Future

	SINGULAR		PLURAL	
FIRST PERSON	poterō	*I will be able*	poterimus	*we will be able*
SECOND PERSON	poteris	*you will be able*	poteritis	*you will be able*
THIRD PERSON	poterit	*he/she/it will be able*	poterunt	*they will be able*

EXERCISE
12·1

Give the correct form of **sum** *or* **possum** *for each of the following verb phrases.*

1. you (*sg.*) were _____

2. he is able _____

3. we are able _____

4. they will be _____

5. you (*sg.*) are able _____

6. we were _____

7. they were able _____

8. he is _____

9. she will be able _____

10. they are _____

EXERCISE
12·2

Identify the person, number, and tense of each of the following verbs.

1. eram _____

2. poterat _____

3. eris _____

4. potest _____

5. erant _____

6. erunt _____

7. sunt _____

8. poterās _____

9. erō _____

10. poterit _____

Keeping the same person and number, transform each of the following present-tense verbs to the imperfect and future.

1. potest _____

2. sunt _____

3. es _____

4. potestis _____

5. possum _____

6. sumus _____

7. potes _____

8. sum _____

9. est _____

10. possunt _____

The present active infinitive

The infinitive is a verb acting as a noun. An infinitive doesn't have person or number, because it expresses the idea of the verb rather than an action by a specific person or thing. It is the abstract version, so to speak, of the verb. Because it is a noun, it can act as the subject or object of a sentence. The usual English translation is to _____.

Legere est hūmānum.	*To read is civilized. / Reading is civilized.*
Amāre est gaudium.	*To love is joy. / Loving is joy.*

In addition, the infinitive frequently serves to complete or fill out the meaning of another verb. This is called the complementary infinitive, and it occurs often with the verb **possum**.

Nōn potest ēvādere.	*He isn't able to escape.*
Poterant dominum invenīre.	*They were able to discover the master.*

The present active infinitive is listed in dictionaries as the second principal part of a verb. The present active infinitive of a regular Latin verb always ends in **-re**.

Translate each of the following phrases featuring complementary infinitives into English.

1. potes excipere _____

2. possunt discēdere _____

3. poterit discere _____

4. reperīre poterant _____

5. potest ardēre _____

6. volāre poteritis _____

7. poterāmus iūrāre _____

8. dēdūcere possum _____

9. praecipere poterō _____

10. poteris vīvere _____

Translate each of the following sentences into English.

1. Mox poterit ad caelum pervenīre.

_____

2. Possunt dēnique agrōs proximōs dīvidere.

_____

3. Rursus dēbent terga vertere.

_____

4. Audēbam discēdere cum librīs tuīs.

_____

5. Quōmodo potes esse fessa?

_____

6. Sine tē vīvere nōn poterō.

_____

7. Possunt vincula nova rumpere.

_____

8. Nōn licet mihi hinc intrāre.

_____

9. Potest tēlō mē occīdere, sī permittis.

_____

10. Poterant membra nōbīs ostendere.

_____

Prepositions and their cases

Prepositional phrases in Latin are used to modify verbs and, sometimes, nouns. They indicate the relationship of a word or phrase to the rest of the sentence. In this way, they are very similar to the cases themselves. Each Latin preposition uses only a particular case (or cases) to show its meaning.

Here are some common prepositions in Latin, with the case(s) each one uses.

PREPOSITION	CASE	MEANING
in	+ acc.	into
	+ abl.	in, on
cum	+ abl.	with
ad	+ acc.	to, toward
ab/ā	+ abl.	from, by
dē	+ abl.	from, about
per	+ acc.	through
ex/ē	+ abl.	out of, from
inter	+ acc.	between, among
sine	+ abl.	without
ante	+ acc.	before
sub	+ acc.	near to
	+ abl.	under
prō	+ abl.	on behalf of
apud	+ acc.	at, at the house of
propter	+ acc.	on account of
prope	+ acc.	near
circā	+ acc.	around
praeter	+ acc.	past, alongside, besides
cōram	+ acc.	in the presence of
ob	+ acc.	on account of
suprā	+ acc.	above
intrā	+ acc.	inside
ultrā	+ acc.	beyond
iuxtā	+ acc.	next to

Translate each of the following prepositional phrases into English.

1. sine ventō _____

2. dē aurō _____

3. ad amīcōs _____

4. in tenebrīs _____

5. in locum _____

6. ex castrīs _____

7. cum equīs _____

8. prope mūrum _____

9. ob sociōs _____

10. per tempus _____

Give the correct form of each of the nouns and pronouns in parentheses.

1. cum _____ (puerī)

2. apud _____ (tū)

3. ex _____ (liber)

4. prō _____ (amīcitiae)

5. ab _____ (imperium)

6. sunt in _____ (Italia)

7. iuxtā _____ (nātus)

8. vocant in _____ (iūdicium)

9. suprā _____ (terrae)

10. ad _____ (astra)

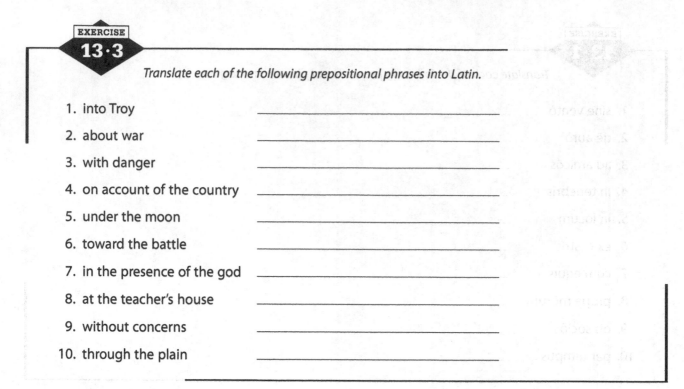

Translate each of the following prepositional phrases into Latin.

1. into Troy _____

2. about war _____

3. with danger _____

4. on account of the country _____

5. under the moon _____

6. toward the battle _____

7. in the presence of the god _____

8. at the teacher's house _____

9. without concerns _____

10. through the plain _____

Third-declension nouns

The third declension introduces another pattern of case endings to indicate the functions of nouns in sentences. As with the first and second declensions, the case endings attach to the stem of the noun, which can be found from the genitive singular form.

The third declension is the largest and most varied group of nouns in Latin. The third declension has no characteristic vowel sound, because most of the stems end in a consonant. No gender predominates: nouns may be masculine, feminine, or neuter. The form of the nominative singular can be difficult to predict (that's the reason for the asterisks in the chart that follows), so you may need to memorize the nominative form of each word. The genitive singular of every third-declension noun ends in -is.

NUMBER	CASE	MASCULINE/ FEMININE	NEUTER
SINGULAR	NOMINATIVE	—*	—*
	GENITIVE	-is	-is
	DATIVE	-ī	-ī
	ACCUSATIVE	-em	—*
	ABLATIVE	-e	-e
	VOCATIVE	—*	—*
PLURAL	NOMINATIVE	-ēs	-a
	GENITIVE	-um	-um
	DATIVE	-ibus	-ibus
	ACCUSATIVE	-ēs	-a
	ABLATIVE	-ibus	-ibus
	VOCATIVE	-ēs	-a

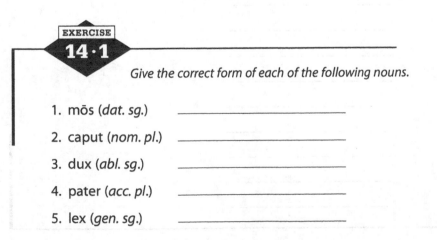

EXERCISE
14·1

Give the correct form of each of the following nouns.

1. mōs (*dat. sg.*) _____

2. caput (*nom. pl.*) _____

3. dux (*abl. sg.*) _____

4. pater (*acc. pl.*) _____

5. lex (*gen. sg.*) _____

6. cīvitās (*gen. pl.*) _____

7. dolor (*nom. pl.*) _____

8. consul (*dat. pl.*) _____

9. aequor (*acc. sg.*) _____

10. iūdex (*abl. pl.*) _____

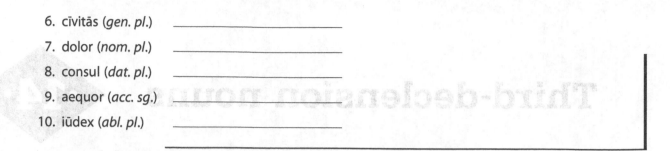

EXERCISE

14·2

List all possible cases for each of the following nouns.

1. homine _____

2. victōrem _____

3. crīminibus _____

4. opēs _____

5. pācī _____

6. legiōnum _____

7. pudōrēs _____

8. coniugem _____

9. matribus _____

10. rēgis _____

EXERCISE

14·3

Give the form of the adjective in parentheses that agrees with each of the following nouns. Some adjectives may have more than one form.

1. (tener tenera tenerum) flōribus _____

2. (optimus -a -um) genera _____

3. (dūrus -a -um) hiemis _____

4. (nocturnus -a -um) pontōs _____

5. (mīrus -a -um) flūmine _____

6. (summus -a -um) lapidī _____

7. (iustus -a -um) senēs _____

8. (paucus -a -um) māteriā _____

9. (aeternus -a -um) laudum _____

10. (ullus -a -um) ratiōnem _____

Third-declension i-stem nouns

There is a subgroup of third-declension nouns that have stems that end in -i. For the most part, this group follows the declension pattern above, but a few of the case endings are different. Here are the declensions of two i-stem nouns:

NUMBER	CASE	MASCULINE/ FEMININE	NEUTER
SINGULAR	NOMINATIVE	pars	mare
	GENITIVE	partis	maris
	DATIVE	partī	marī
	ACCUSATIVE	partem	mare
	ABLATIVE	parte	marī
	VOCATIVE	pars	mare
PLURAL	NOMINATIVE	partēs	maria
	GENITIVE	partium	marium
	DATIVE	partibus	maribus
	ACCUSATIVE	partēs	maria
	ABLATIVE	partibus	maribus
	VOCATIVE	partēs	maria

Identifying i-stem nouns

It can be difficult to tell whether a third-declension noun is an i-stem or not; however, i-stems usually fall into one of the following categories.

1. A nominative singular and genitive singular with the same number of syllables (and the nominative singular often ending in -is)
2. A one-syllable nominative singular and a genitive singular with two consonants before -is (and the nominative singular often ending in -s or -x)
3. A nominative singular of a neuter noun that ends in -al, -ar, or -e.

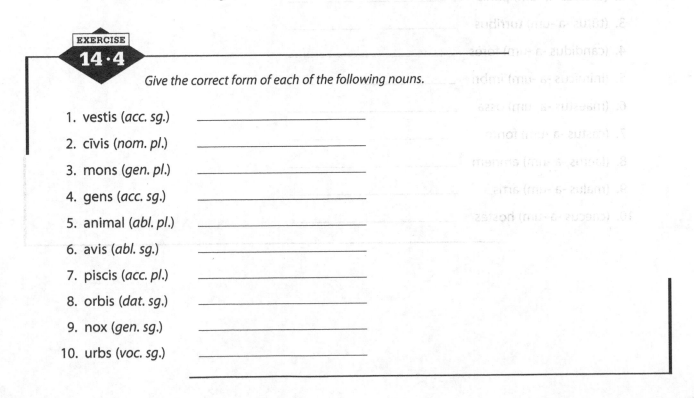

EXERCISE 14·4

Give the correct form of each of the following nouns.

1. vestis (*acc. sg.*) _____
2. cīvis (*nom. pl.*) _____
3. mons (*gen. pl.*) _____
4. gens (*acc. sg.*) _____
5. animal (*abl. pl.*) _____
6. avis (*abl. sg.*) _____
7. piscis (*acc. pl.*) _____
8. orbis (*dat. sg.*) _____
9. nox (*gen. sg.*) _____
10. urbs (*voc. sg.*) _____

List all possible cases for each of the following nouns.

1. ovēs _____

2. arce _____

3. nāvī _____

4. maria _____

5. mortibus _____

6. nivem _____

7. mentium _____

8. sorte _____

9. caedēs _____

10. fīnis _____

Give the form of the adjective in parentheses that agrees with each of the following nouns.
Some adjectives may have more than one form.

1. (saevus -a -um) ignium _____

2. (cēterus -a -um) pānis _____

3. (tūtus -a -um) turribus _____

4. (candidus -a -um) forēs _____

5. (inimīcus -a -um) imbrī _____

6. (maestus -a -um) ossa _____

7. (castus -a -um) fonte _____

8. (laetus -a -um) amnem _____

9. (malus -a -um) artis _____

10. (caecus -a -um) hostēs _____

Common third-declension nouns

aequor, aequoris (n.)	sea	hiems, hiemis (f.)	winter
aes, aeris (n.)	money	homō, hominis (m.)	man
aetās, aetātis (f.)	age	honor, honōris (m.)	honor
aethēr, aetheris (m.)	sky	hospes, hospitis (m.)	guest
agmen, agminis (n.)	herd	hostis, hostis (m.)	enemy
amnis, amnis (m.)	river	ignis, ignis (m.)	fire
amor, amōris (m.)	love	imāgō, imāginis (f.)	image
animal, animālis (n.)	animal	imber, imbris (m.)	shower
Apollō, Apollinis (m.)	Apollo	imperātor, imperātōris (m.)	emperor
arbor, arboris (f.)	tree	iter, itineris (n.)	journey
ars, artis (f.)	art	iūdex, iūdicis (m.)	judge
arx, arcis (f.)	citadel	Iuppiter, Iovis (m.)	Jupiter
auctor, auctōris (m.)	founder, author	iūs, iūris (n.)	law
auris, auris (f.)	ear	iuvenis, iuvenis (m./f.)	youth
avis, avis (f.)	bird	labor, labōris (m.)	work
caedēs, caedis (f.)	slaughter	lapis, lapidis (m.)	stone
Caesar, Caesaris (m.)	Caesar	laus, laudis (f.)	praise
canis, canis (m./f.)	dog	legiō, legiōnis (f.)	legion
caput, capitis (n.)	head	leō, leōnis (m.)	lion
carmen, carminis (n.)	song	lex, lēgis (f.)	law
cinis, cineris (m.)	ash	līmen, līminis (n.)	threshhold
cīvis, cīvis (m./f.)	citizen	lītus, lītoris (n.)	shore
cīvitās, cīvitātis (f.)	state	lūmen, lūminis (n.)	light
clāmor, clāmōris (m.)	shouting	lux, lūcis (f.)	light
cohors, cohortis (f.)	cohort	magnitūdō, magnitūdinis (f.)	size
color, colōris (m.)	color	mare, maris (n.)	sea
comes, comitis (m./f.)	companion	Mars, Martis (m.)	Mars
coniunx, coniugis (f.)	wife	māter, matris (f.)	mother
consul, consulis (m.)	consul	mens, mentis (f.)	mind
cor, cordis (n.)	heart	mīles, mīlitis (m.)	soldier
corpus, corporis (n.)	body	mons, montis (m.)	mountain
crīmen, crīminis (n.)	charge	mors, mortis (f.)	death
cupīdō, cupīdinis (m./f.)	desire	mōs, mōris (m.)	custom
custōs, custōdis (m./f.)	guardian	mulier, mulieris (f.)	wife
decus, decoris (n.)	beauty	multitūdō, multitūdinis (f.)	multitude
dignitās, dignitātis (f.)	dignity	mūnus, mūneris (n.)	service
dolor, dolōris (m.)	pain	nāvis, nāvis (f.)	ship
dux, ducis (m.)	leader	necessitās, necessitātis (f.)	need
eques, equitis (m.)	equestrian	nēmō, nēminis (m.)	no one
famēs, famis (f.)	hunger	nemus, nemoris (n.)	woods
fax, facis (f.)	torch	nix, nivis (f.)	snow
fīnis, fīnis (m.)	limit	nōmen, nōminis (n.)	name
flōs, flōris (m.)	flower	nox, noctis (f.)	night
flūmen, flūminis (n.)	river	nūmen, nūminis (n.)	divinity
fons, fontis (m.)	fountain	ops, opis (f.)	resources
foris, foris (f.)	door	opus, operis (n.)	work
frāter, fratris (m.)	brother	ōrātiō, ōrātiōnis (f.)	speech
frons, frontis (f.)	brow	orbis, orbis (m.)	circle
fūnus, fūneris (n.)	funeral	ordō, ordinis (m.)	rank
gens, gentis (f.)	clan	ōs, ōris (n.)	mouth
genus, generis (n.)	kind	os, ossis (n.)	bone

ovis, ovis (f.)	sheep	sēdēs, sēdis (f.)	seat
pānis, pānis (m.)	bread	senex, senis (m.)	old man
parens, parentis (m./f.)	parent	sermō, sermōnis (m.)	conversation
pars, partis (f.)	part	sīdus, sīderis (n.)	star
pater, patris (m.)	father	sōl, sōlis (m.)	sun
pax, pācis (f.)	peace	soror, sorōris (f.)	sister
pectus, pectoris (n.)	chest	sors, sortis (f.)	fate
pēs, pedis (m.)	foot	tellūs, tellūris (f.)	earth
pietās, pietātis (f.)	piety	tempus, temporis (n.)	time
piscis, piscis (m.)	fish	timor, timōris (m.)	fear
plūs, plūris (n.)	more	turris, turris (f.)	tower
pondus, ponderis (n.)	weight	urbs, urbis (f.)	city
potestās, potestātis (f.)	ability	uxor, uxōris (f.)	wife
prex, precis (f.)	prayer	vātēs, vātis (m.)	prophet
princeps, principis (m.)	leader	Venus, Veneris (f.)	Venus
pudor, pudōris (m.)	modesty	vēr, vēris (n.)	spring
ratiō, ratiōnis (f.)	reason, account	vestis, vestis (f.)	clothing
regiō, regiōnis (f.)	region	victor, victōris (m.)	winner
rex, rēgis (m.)	king	virgō, virginis (f.)	young woman
rūs, rūris (n.)	farm	virtūs, virtūtis (f.)	virtue
sacerdōs, sacerdōtis (m.)	priest	vīs, (vīr-) (f.)	strength
salūs, salūtis (f.)	health	voluptās, voluptātis (f.)	pleasure
sanguis, sanguinis (m.)	blood	vox, vōcis (f.)	voice
scelus, sceleris (n.)	crime	vulnus, vulneris (n.)	wound

Third-declension adjectives

You have already learned the case endings of **-us -a -um** adjectives. The other major group of adjectives in Latin is third-declension adjectives. Just as **-us -a -um** adjectives use the same case endings as first- and second-declension nouns, third-declension adjectives use the same case endings as third-declension **i**-stem nouns. Even though these adjectives have a new pattern of endings, third-declension adjectives must still have the same case, number, and gender as the nouns they describe.

With two different groups of adjectives and three different groups of nouns, you will often see that an adjective's case ending does not always echo the ending of the noun it modifies. For example, a noun that has the genitive case ending **-ae** may be modified by an adjective that ends in **-ae** or one that ends in **-is**.

Nominative forms

There are three subgroups of third-declension adjectives, distinguished by the number of nominative forms: separate nominative forms for masculine, feminine, and neuter (three-ending), one nominative form for masculine and feminine and a different one for neuter (two-ending—the most common type), and one nominative form for masculine, feminine, and neuter (one-ending—the least common type). Except for the nominative singular, there is no distinction between the three groups.

Here are examples of third-declension adjectives:

Three-ending

NUMBER	CASE	MASCULINE	FEMININE	NEUTER
SINGULAR	NOMINATIVE	volucer	volucris	volucre
	GENITIVE	volucris	volucris	volucris
	DATIVE	volucrī	volucrī	volucrī
	ACCUSATIVE	volucrem	volucrem	volucre
	ABLATIVE	volucrī	volucrī	volucrī
	VOCATIVE	volucer	volucris	volucre
PLURAL	NOMINATIVE	volucrēs	volucrēs	volucria
	GENITIVE	volucrium	volucrium	volucrium
	DATIVE	volucribus	volucribus	volucribus
	ACCUSATIVE	volucrēs	volucrēs	volucria
	ABLATIVE	volucribus	volucribus	volucribus
	VOCATIVE	volucrēs	volucrēs	volucria

Two-ending

NUMBER	CASE	MASCULINE/ FEMININE	NEUTER
SINGULAR	NOMINATIVE	omnis	omne
	GENITIVE	omnis	omnis
	DATIVE	omnī	omnī
	ACCUSATIVE	omnem	omne
	ABLATIVE	omnī	omnī
	VOCATIVE	omnis	omne
PLURAL	NOMINATIVE	omnēs	omnia
	GENITIVE	omnium	omnium
	DATIVE	omnibus	omnibus
	ACCUSATIVE	omnēs	omnia
	ABLATIVE	omnibus	omnibus
	VOCATIVE	omnēs	omnia

One-ending

NUMBER	CASE	MASCULINE/ FEMININE	NEUTER
SINGULAR	NOMINATIVE	fēlix	fēlix
	GENITIVE	fēlīcis	fēlīcis
	DATIVE	fēlīcī	fēlīcī
	ACCUSATIVE	fēlīcem	fēlix
	ABLATIVE	fēlīcī	fēlīcī
	VOCATIVE	fēlix	fēlix
PLURAL	NOMINATIVE	fēlīcēs	fēlīcia
	GENITIVE	fēlīcium	fēlīcium
	DATIVE	fēlīcibus	fēlīcibus
	ACCUSATIVE	fēlīcēs	fēlīcia
	ABLATIVE	fēlīcibus	fēlīcibus
	VOCATIVE	fēlīcēs	fēlīcia

The neuter forms differ from the masculine/feminine forms only in the accusative singular and the nominative, accusative, and vocative plural.

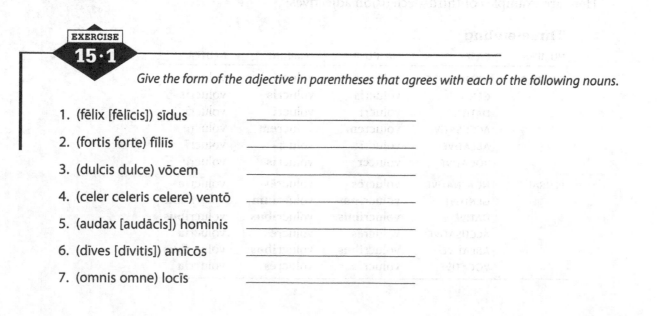

EXERCISE

15·1

Give the form of the adjective in parentheses that agrees with each of the following nouns.

1. (fēlix [fēlīcis]) sīdus _____

2. (fortis forte) fīliīs _____

3. (dulcis dulce) vōcem _____

4. (celer celeris celere) ventō _____

5. (audax [audācis]) hominis _____

6. (dīves [dīvitis]) amīcōs _____

7. (omnis omne) locīs _____

8. (brevis breve) īrās _____

9. (tālis tāle) formā _____

10. (turpis turpe) vulnere _____

EXERCISE
15·2

Keeping the same case, transform each of the following adjectives into its opposite number, singular to plural or plural to singular. Some adjectives may have more than one opposite-number form.

1. ingentēs _____   6. praesentem _____

2. fidēlibus _____   7. parī _____

3. acris _____   8. mortālis _____

4. sublīme _____   9. triste _____

5. ūtilium _____   10. similia _____

EXERCISE
15·3

From the following adjective-noun phrases, choose those in which the adjectives agree properly with their nouns.

pauperem iuvenem	potens Trōia	āles avēs	facilī labōrī
nōbilēs rēgem	omnēs hominis	volucrī somnō	caelestibus deīs
sapientium iūdicum	insignis animae	magnam partem	inānibus animōs
mītem patrem	gravia vōta	levēs causās	veterium patriam
mollia opera	dīligentis uxorī	commūnī mundō	frequentibus populīs

EXERCISE
15·4

Translate each of the following adjective-noun phrases into Latin.

1. our boys (*acc. pl.*) _____

2. miserable money (*abl. sg.*) _____

3. whole cohort (*dat. pl.*) _____

4. thankful soldier (*nom. pl.*) _____

5. huge farm (*acc. sg.*) _____

6. eminent light (*acc. pl.*) _____

7. wicked slave (*gen. sg.*) _____

8. worried prayer (*dat. sg.*) _____

9. good life (*gen. pl.*) _____

10. lucky young woman (*abl. pl.*) _____

EXERCISE

15·5

Translate each of the following sentences into English.

1. Littera veniēbat in mentem meam.

_____

2. Urbs vestra est mihi patria.

_____

3. Castra hostium continēbunt multās cohortēs.

_____

4. Nec trādere nec accipere possum tālem pecūniam.

_____

5. Ō deī, genus hūmānum poenīs regitis.

_____

6. Consulem aegrum vōtīs iuvāmus.

_____

7. Obvius erat Gallus in equō nōbilī.

_____

8. Ventus corpus dūcēbat sub undīs.

_____

9. Numquam sūmet consilia nova.

_____

10. Deinde mē occīditis in convīviō, saevī amīcī!

_____

Common third-declension adjectives

Three-ending adjectives

ācer acris acre	*sharp*
celer celeris celere	*swift*
volucer volucris volucre	*swift*

Two-ending adjectives

brevis breve	*brief*	mollis molle	*soft*
caelestis caeleste	*heavenly*	mortālis mortāle	*mortal*
commūnis commūne	*common*	nōbilis nōbile	*noble*
dulcis dulce	*sweet*	omnis omne	*all, every*
facilis facile	*easy*	potis pote	*able*
fidēlis fidēle	*faithful*	quālis quāle	*what kind*
fortis forte	*strong*	similis simile	*similar*
gravis grave	*heavy*	sublīmis sublīme	*lofty*
inānis ināne	*empty*	tālis tāle	*such*
insignis insigne	*eminent*	tristis triste	*sad*
levis leve	*light*	turpis turpe	*foul*
mītis mīte	*mild*	ūtilis ūtile	*useful*

One-ending adjectives

āles (ālitis)	*winged*	memor (memoris)	*remembering*
audax (audācis)	*bold*	pār (paris)	*equal*
dīligens (dīligentis)	*careful*	pauper (pauperis)	*poor*
dīves (dīvitis)	*rich*	potens (potentis)	*powerful*
fēlix (fēlīcis)	*lucky*	praesens (praesentis)	*present*
frequens (frequentis)	*crowded*	sapiens (sapientis)	*wise*
ingens (ingentis)	*huge*	vetus (veteris)	*old*
libens (libentis)	*willing*		

·16· Fourth-declension nouns

The fourth declension is built around the sound -**u**-. Be careful not to confuse these nouns with second-declension nouns, whose nominative singular also ends in -**us**; the genitive singular of fourth-declension nouns ends in -**ūs**, and they have a different pattern of case endings in the remaining cases. Nonetheless, the fourth declension forms nouns like the other declensions: the case endings are added to the noun stem, which is found in the genitive singular.

Fourth-declension nouns are much rarer than nouns of the first three declensions, although a few of them are very common. Most of them are masculine, but a few are feminine or neuter. Here is the pattern of case endings for the fourth declension:

NUMBER	CASE	MASCULINE/ FEMININE	NEUTER
SINGULAR	NOMINATIVE	-us	-ū
	GENITIVE	-ūs	-ūs
	DATIVE	-uī	-ū
	ACCUSATIVE	-um	-ū
	ABLATIVE	-ū	-ū
	VOCATIVE	-us	-ū
PLURAL	NOMINATIVE	-ūs	-ua
	GENITIVE	-uum	-uum
	DATIVE	-ibus	-ibus
	ACCUSATIVE	-ūs	-ua
	ABLATIVE	-ibus	-ibus
	VOCATIVE	-ūs	-ua

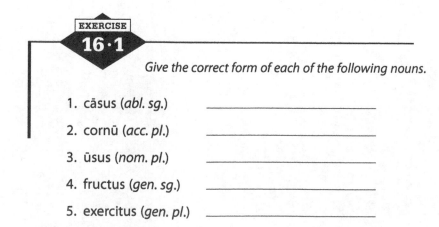

EXERCISE

16·1

Give the correct form of each of the following nouns.

1. cāsus (*abl. sg.*) _____

2. cornū (*acc. pl.*) _____

3. ūsus (*nom. pl.*) _____

4. fructus (*gen. sg.*) _____

5. exercitus (*gen. pl.*) _____

6. domus (*acc. sg.*) _____

7. vultus (*abl. pl.*) _____

8. spīritus (*voc. sg.*) _____

9. cantus (*dat. sg.*) _____

10. lacus (*dat. pl.*) _____

EXERCISE
16·2

List all possible cases for each of the following nouns.

1. manibus _____

2. cāsūs _____

3. metum _____

4. cornuum _____

5. sinū _____

6. vultuī _____

7. fructus _____

8. cursibus _____

9. exercitūs _____

10. versum _____

EXERCISE
16·3

Give the form of the adjective in parentheses that agrees with each of the following nouns.
Some adjectives may have more than one form.

1. (perpetuus -a -um) metūs _____

2. (mollis molle) fructuum _____

3. (niger nigra nigrum) lacibus _____

4. (superbus -a -um) vultū _____

5. (blandus -a -um) cantuī _____

6. (aureus -a -um) domūs _____

7. (insignis insigne) versum _____

8. (facilis facile) manus _____

9. (tardus -a -um) cornūs _____

10. (magnus -a -um) sinuī _____

Translate each of the following phrases into Latin.

1. the whole army (*abl.*) _____

2. soft hands (*nom.*) _____

3. varied falls (*acc.*) _____

4. heavy fear (*dat.*) _____

5. beautiful face (*gen.*) _____

6. such fruit (*acc.*) _____

7. long horn (*gen.*) _____

8. famous song (*dat.*) _____

9. our house (*nom.*) _____

10. wide lake (*abl.*) _____

VOCABULARY

Common fourth-declension nouns

cantus, cantūs (*m.*)	song		manus, manūs (*f.*)	hand
cāsus, cāsūs (*m.*)	fall		metus, metūs (*m.*)	fear
cornū, cornūs (*n.*)	horn		sensus, sensūs (*m.*)	feeling
cursus, cursūs (*m.*)	race		sinus, sinūs (*m.*)	fold
domus, domūs (*f.*)	house		spīritus, spīritūs (*m.*)	breath
exercitus, exercitūs (*m.*)	army		ūsus, ūsūs (*m.*)	use
fructus, fructūs (*m.*)	fruit		versus, versūs (*m.*)	verse
lacus, lacūs (*m.*)	lake		vultus, vultūs (*m.*)	face

Fifth-declension nouns

The fifth declension is the last noun declension and the last new pattern of case endings. It is built around the sound **-e-**. Fifth-declension nouns are rarer than nouns of the first three declensions, although a few of them are very common.

Most fifth-declension nouns are feminine. All of them have a genitive singular ending in **-eī** or **-ēī**. Here is the pattern of case endings for the fifth declension:

NUMBER	CASE	ENDING
SINGULAR	NOMINATIVE	-ēs
	GENITIVE	-eī
	DATIVE	-eī
	ACCUSATIVE	-em
	ABLATIVE	-ē
	VOCATIVE	-ēs
PLURAL	NOMINATIVE	-ēs
	GENITIVE	-ērum
	DATIVE	-ēbus
	ACCUSATIVE	-ēs
	ABLATIVE	-ēbus
	VOCATIVE	-ēs

EXERCISE

17·1

Give the correct form of each of the following nouns.

1. rēs (*acc. sg.*) _____

2. diēs (*nom. pl.*) _____

3. fidēs (*gen. sg.*) _____

4. spēs (*dat. sg.*) _____

5. aciēs (*acc. pl.*) _____

6. faciēs (*nom. pl.*) _____

7. rēs (*abl. sg.*) _____

8. diēs (*acc. sg.*) _____

9. speciēs (*gen. pl.*) _____

10. fidēs (*dat. pl.*) _____

List all possible cases for each of the following nouns.

1. fidēī _____

2. rēs _____

3. speciem _____

4. diēbus _____

5. rē _____

6. faciēs _____

7. spērum _____

8. rērum _____

9. aciem _____

10. diēs _____

Give the form of the adjective in parentheses that agrees with each of the following nouns. Some adjectives may have more than one form.

1. (paucus -a -um) rem _____

2. (vērus -a -um) fidērum _____

3. (medius -a -um) aciēs _____

4. (Latīnus -a -um) reī _____

5. (vīvus -a -um) faciem _____

6. (omnis omne) diē _____

7. (potens [potentis]) spem _____

8. (tristis triste) diem _____

9. (quālis quāle) faciēbus _____

10. (mortālis mortāle) specieī _____

Translate each of the following phrases into Latin.

1. good things (*acc.*) _____

2. blind faith (*gen.*) _____

3. lucky day (*gen.*) _____

4. foul appearance (*dat.*) _____

5. pleasant things (*nom.*) _____

6. new thing (*abl.*) _____

7. no point (*abl.*) _____

8. closest day (*nom.*) _____

9. doubtful hope (*acc.*) _____

10. wonderful face (*abl.*) _____

VOCABULARY

Common fifth-declension nouns

aciēs, aciēī (*f.*)	*point*	rēs, reī (*f.*)	*thing*
diēs, diēī (*m.*)	*day*	speciēs, speciēī (*f.*)	*appearance*
faciēs, faciēī (*f.*)	*face*	spēs, speī (*f.*)	*hope*
fidēs, fidēī (*f.*)	*faith*		

Substantive adjectives

Adjectives may be used for a purpose other than modifying nouns. An adjective may itself function as a noun; in this case, it is considered a substantive adjective.

> the good, the bad, and the ugly
> = the good [people], the bad [people], and the ugly [people]

When a Latin adjective is used as a substantive, the gender of the case ending indicates whether the adjective refers to a male (if the adjective is masculine), a female (if it's feminine), or a thing (if it's neuter). Adjectives are commonly used in this way in Latin, because it is conveniently concise, while still conveying all the necessary information.

mōs maiōrum	*the custom of the elders*
vēra	*true things*

You encountered the noun **rēs**, meaning *thing*, in the previous chapter, but in many circumstances, Latin uses a neuter substantive adjective to mean *thing*—not the word **rēs**.

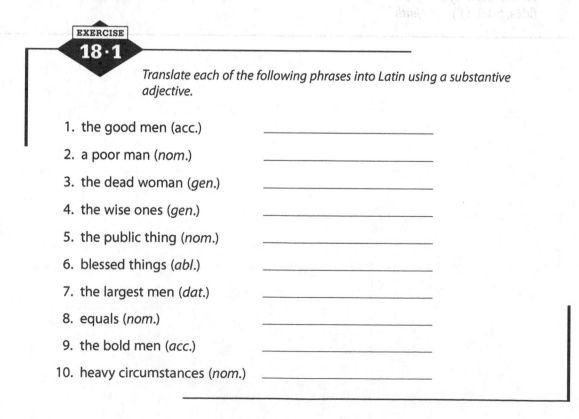

EXERCISE

18·1

Translate each of the following phrases into Latin using a substantive adjective.

1. the good men (acc.) _____

2. a poor man (*nom.*) _____

3. the dead woman (*gen.*) _____

4. the wise ones (*gen.*) _____

5. the public thing (*nom.*) _____

6. blessed things (*abl.*) _____

7. the largest men (*dat.*) _____

8. equals (*nom.*) _____

9. the bold men (*acc.*) _____

10. heavy circumstances (*nom.*) _____

9. Cur pecūniās reddimus sapientibus?

10. Itaque sit nostram sententiam.

EXERCISE 18·2

Translate each of the following substantive adjectives into English.

1. vetera _____

2. multōs _____

3. sacrīs _____

4. prīmīs _____

5. antīquōrum _____

6. Graecī _____

7. volucrēs _____

8. meōs _____

9. proximō _____

10. adversīs _____

EXERCISE 18·3

Translate each of the following sentences into English.

1. Reliquī tamen famem sentiēbant.

_____

2. Improbus iam dē scelere cōgitat.

_____

3. Paucī sunt dīvitēs.

_____

4. Dīvī monent enim ab aquā aut ab ignī perīcula.

_____

5. Magnum animum in adversīs habēre dēbēbās.

_____

6. Nēmō mihi erit similis.

_____

7. Rēs ipsa nōs docēbit.

_____

8. Rusticī rapient causās inānēs.

_____

9. Cūr pecūniās reddimus sapientibus?

_____

10. Itaque scīs nostram sententiam.

_____

More uses of the ablative

So far, you have seen the ablative used primarily as the object of a preposition. But the ablative encompasses several adverbial uses in Latin. These uses can be grouped into three categories that correspond with three fundamental notions that coalesced in Latin's ablative case.

1. Motion away from
2. Location in a spot
3. Association with

If you understand these three categories, it will make sense that the ablative is used with the prepositions **dē**, **ab**, and **ex** (1), with **in** meaning *in a place* but not *into* (2), and with **cum** (3).

But there are also extended, more metaphorical instances of these three basic notions that Latin uses with or without prepositions. Here are some common ones:

Motion away from

Place from which

Ex **Italiā** discēdit.	*He departs from Italy.*
Domō abit.	*He leaves his house.*

Separation

Metū mē līberat.	*He frees me from fear.*

Origin or material

Templum **aurō** pōnam.	*I will put up a temple of gold.*

Agent with passive verbs

ab **Augustō** rogātus	*having been asked by Augustus*

Location in a spot

Place where

In **campō** pugnāmus.	*We are fighting on the plain.*
Proeliīs pereunt.	*They are dying in the battles.*

Association with

Means

> **Tēlīs gladiīsque** urbem dēfendimus.   *We are defending the city with spears and swords.*

Manner

> **Magnā sapientiā** consilium capiet.   *With great wisdom, he will come up with a plan.*

Description

> Gallia est patria **vērā dignitāte**.   *Gaul is a country of true dignity.*

Specification

> Mē superat **glōriā**, nōn **victōriīs**.   *He outdoes me in glory, but not in victories.*

It can be difficult to distinguish these uses of the ablative, because nothing explicitly marks the distinction between them. In these cases, make sure you understand precisely what sense each usage of the ablative expresses, and let the context of the rest of the sentence help you.

EXERCISE 19·1

Identify which use of the Latin ablative would express the italicized phrase in each of the following sentences.

1. They ran *from the jail*. _____

2. The bull gored him *with its horns*. _____

3. They were young men *of great promise*. _____

4. He is your superior *in name only*. _____

5. Do you have a shirt made *of linen*? _____

6. She drenched her sleeve *with tears*. _____

7. The horse was ridden *by a tall man*. _____

8. They finally found me *in the park*. _____

9. At the end of the month, my roommate was lacking *money*. _____

10. Mars caught sight of him *with his eyes*. _____

EXERCISE 19·2

Translate each of the following sentences into English.

1. Versūs tunc arte carēbant.

_____

2. Omnī cūrā perficis tōtum.

_____

3. Fīlius pauca ossa matris ex igne rapiet.

_____

4. Aliōs dōnīs ad meam causam dēducō.

_____

5. Famulus cum summō studiō in agrīs labōrābat.

_____

6. Ferrō dīvīnō gladius est.

_____

7. Ingentī pondere saxa iaciēbāmus.

_____

8. Mīlitēs nullā virtūte fugere temptant.

_____

9. Cūr vīvunt hominēs in nāvibus per aetātem?

_____

10. Poētae mollī cantū certāre incipiunt.

_____

The perfect tense

The perfect tense can express either of two ideas about the time of a verb:

1. An action performed instantaneously in the past (the simple perfect). The usual English translation is _____*ed*.

2. An action performed in the past and completed as of right now (the present perfect). The usual English translation is *have/has* _____*ed*. The following sentence illustrates both of these ideas.

> I have read everything you asked me to.

Have read describes a present state resulting from the completion of a past action (2), while *asked* describes a simple action that occurred in the past (1).

Forming the perfect tense

The perfect tense is formed from a different root than the present, imperfect, and future tenses are; it is formed from the perfect active system root. To this root is added a special set of perfect active personal endings, which are not used for any other tense. The conjugation of every verb, including irregular verbs, is the same in the perfect tense. Here is the formula for the perfect tense:

> Perfect active system root + Perfect active personal endings = Perfect tense

To find the perfect active system root of any verb, drop the **-ī** ending of the third principal part; what's left is the root.

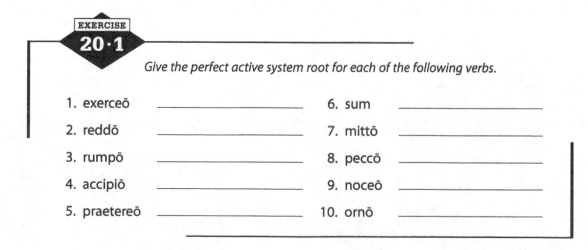

EXERCISE

20·1

Give the perfect active system root for each of the following verbs.

1. exerceō _____
2. reddō _____
3. rumpō _____
4. accipiō _____
5. praetereō _____

6. sum _____
7. mittō _____
8. peccō _____
9. noceō _____
10. ornō _____

Following are the perfect active personal endings. (You'll notice some similarities to the personal endings you already know.)

	SINGULAR	PLURAL
FIRST PERSON	-ī	-imus
SECOND PERSON	-istī	-istis
THIRD PERSON	-it	-ērunt

Here are example charts of the perfect tense for each conjugation:

First conjugation

amō, amāre, amāvī, amātum *love*
PERFECT ACTIVE SYSTEM ROOT   amāv-

	SINGULAR		PLURAL	
FIRST PERSON	amāvī	*I loved*	amāvimus	*we loved*
SECOND PERSON	amāvistī	*you loved*	amāvistis	*you loved*
THIRD PERSON	amāvit	*he/she/it loved*	amāvērunt	*they loved*

Second conjugation

teneō, tenēre, tenuī, tentum *hold*
PERFECT ACTIVE SYSTEM ROOT   tenu-

	SINGULAR		PLURAL	
FIRST PERSON	tenuī	*I held*	tenuimus	*we held*
SECOND PERSON	tenuistī	*you held*	tenuistis	*you held*
THIRD PERSON	tenuit	*he/she/it held*	tenuērunt	*they held*

Third conjugation

pōnō, pōnere, posuī, positum *put*
PERFECT ACTIVE SYSTEM ROOT   posu-

	SINGULAR		PLURAL	
FIRST PERSON	posuī	*I put*	posuimus	*we put*
SECOND PERSON	posuistī	*you put*	posuistis	*you put*
THIRD PERSON	posuit	*he/she/it put*	posuērunt	*they put*

Third -iō conjugation

capiō, capere, cēpī, captum *take*
PERFECT ACTIVE SYSTEM ROOT   cēp-

	SINGULAR		PLURAL	
FIRST PERSON	cēpī	*I took*	cēpimus	*we took*
SECOND PERSON	cēpistī	*you took*	cēpistis	*you took*
THIRD PERSON	cēpit	*he/she/it took*	cēpērunt	*they took*

Fourth conjugation

audiō, audīre, audīvī, audītum *hear*
PERFECT ACTIVE SYSTEM ROOT   audīv-

	SINGULAR		PLURAL	
FIRST PERSON	audīvī	*I heard*	audīvimus	*we heard*
SECOND PERSON	audīvistī	*you heard*	audīvistis	*you heard*
THIRD PERSON	audīvit	*he/she/it heard*	audīvērunt	*they heard*

Identify the person, number, and tense of each of the following verbs.

1. miscent _____

2. iacēbant _____

3. cūrant _____

4. potuit _____

5. iussistī _____

6. noscit _____

7. sparsit _____

8. conspexī _____

9. tetigērunt _____

10. impōnent _____

Give the correct form of each of the following verbs.

1. instruō (*1 pl. perfect*) _____

2. colligō (*3 pl. imperfect*) _____

3. exspectō (*2 sg. perfect*) _____

4. videō (*3 sg. present*) _____

5. possum (*3 pl. perfect*) _____

6. servō (*3 pl. future*) _____

7. iūrō (*1 sg. perfect*) _____

8. conveniō (*3 sg. present*) _____

9. gignō (*2 pl. perfect*) _____

10. faciō (*1 sg. perfect*) _____

20·4

Keeping the same person and number, transform each of the following imperfect-tense verbs to the perfect.

1. requīrēbās _____
2. legēbat _____
3. dēcipiēbant _____
4. audiēbam _____
5. currēbāmus _____

6. movēbat _____
7. inveniēbās _____
8. pōnēbat _____
9. creābant _____
10. timēbātis _____

20·5

Translate each of the following verbs into English.

1. compārāvit _____
2. tenēbāmus _____
3. quaerent _____
4. clausistī _____
5. convertērunt _____
6. ēripuistis _____
7. prōpōnis _____
8. pressit _____
9. dīcit _____
10. aperuimus _____

20·6

Translate each of the following verb phrases into Latin.

1. we have compelled _____
2. they brought back _____
3. we will teach _____
4. he has carried _____
5. she was loosening _____

6. you (*pl.*) carried _____

7. you (*sg.*) allow _____

8. he discerned _____

9. they will stray _____

10. it is increasing _____

The pluperfect
and future perfect tenses

Two other tenses are formed from the same root as the perfect tense: the pluperfect and the future perfect. These tenses appear less frequently than the tenses you've already learned, but they are more common in Latin than they are in English.

The pluperfect tense

The pluperfect tense expresses an action that has already been completed at some point in the past. The usual English translation is *had _____ed*.

>When you came into the room, I had finished my project.

In this sentence, *I had finished* was already completed when the past action *you came* occurred.

>Here is the formula for the pluperfect tense:

>>Perfect active system root + Imperfect of **sum** = Pluperfect tense

The conjugation of every verb, including irregular verbs, is the same in the pluperfect tense.

>On the following page are example charts of the pluperfect tense for each conjugation.

First conjugation

amō, amāre, amāvī, amātum *love*
PERFECT ACTIVE SYSTEM ROOT   amāv-

	SINGULAR		PLURAL	
FIRST PERSON	amāveram	*I had loved*	amāverāmus	*we had loved*
SECOND PERSON	amāverās	*you had loved*	amāverātis	*you had loved*
THIRD PERSON	amāverat	*he/she/it had loved*	amāverant	*they had loved*

Second conjugation

habeō, habēre, habuī, habitum *have*
PERFECT ACTIVE SYSTEM ROOT   habu-

	SINGULAR		PLURAL	
FIRST PERSON	habueram	*I had had*	habuerāmus	*we had had*
SECOND PERSON	habuerās	*you had had*	habuerātis	*you had had*
THIRD PERSON	habuerat	*he/she/it had had*	habuerant	*they had had*

Third conjugation

agō, agere, ēgī, actum *drive, act*
PERFECT ACTIVE SYSTEM ROOT   ēg-

	SINGULAR		PLURAL	
FIRST PERSON	ēgeram	*I had driven*	ēgerāmus	*we had driven*
SECOND PERSON	ēgerās	*you had driven*	ēgerātis	*you had driven*
THIRD PERSON	ēgerat	*he/she/it had driven*	ēgerant	*they had driven*

Third -iō conjugation

capiō, capere, cēpī, captum *take*
PERFECT ACTIVE SYSTEM ROOT   cēp-

	SINGULAR		PLURAL	
FIRST PERSON	cēperam	*I had taken*	cēperāmus	*we had taken*
SECOND PERSON	cēperās	*you had taken*	cēperātis	*you had taken*
THIRD PERSON	cēperat	*he/she/it had taken*	cēperant	*they had taken*

Fourth conjugation

audiō, audīre, audīvī, audītum *hear*
PERFECT ACTIVE SYSTEM ROOT   audīv-

	SINGULAR		PLURAL	
FIRST PERSON	audīveram	*I had heard*	audīverāmus	*we had heard*
SECOND PERSON	audīverās	*you had heard*	audīverātis	*you had heard*
THIRD PERSON	audīverat	*he/she/it had heard*	audīverant	*they had heard*

EXERCISE

21·1

Identify the person, number, and tense of each of the following verbs.

1. habēbam _____

2. petīverant _____

3. cecidistī _____

4. rogāvērunt _____

5. dīrexerant _____

6. concēdit _____

7. appellābit _____

8. dēfendēmus _____

9. studuerās _____

10. fluxistis _____

EXERCISE

21·2

Give the correct form of each of the following verbs.

1. placeō (*1 sg. pluperfect*) _____

2. pandō (*2 pl. present*) _____

3. ardeō (*3 pl. pluperfect*) _____

4. sciō (*3 sg. pluperfect*) _____

5. tollō (*2 pl. perfect*) _____

6. volō volāre (*1 sg. pluperfect*) _____

7. canō (*3 pl. pluperfect*) _____

8. retineō (*3 sg. future*) _____

9. incipiō (*2 sg. pluperfect*) _____

10. discō (*3 pl. pluperfect*) _____

Keeping the same person and number, transform each of the following present-tense verbs to the pluperfect.

1. suscipiunt _____

2. cēdis _____

3. respondēmus _____

4. spērō _____

5. cavēs _____

6. contemnitis _____

7. frangit _____

8. vertimus _____

9. aperīs _____

10. existimat _____

Translate each of the following verbs into English.

1. constiterat _____

2. finxērunt _____

3. gaudēbis _____

4. efficit _____

5. composuerāmus _____

6. iūverātis _____

7. ēlēgeram _____

8. fefellerant _____

9. probāvistī _____

10. līquit _____

Translate each of the following verb phrases into Latin.

1. we had escaped _____

2. you (*pl.*) had entrusted _____

3. it had lacked _____

4. they had suffered _____

5. he had given as a gift _____

6. she had demanded _____

7. we had filled _____

8. they had come _____

9. you (*sg.*) had brought in _____

10. I had been able _____

The future perfect tense

The future perfect tense expresses an action that will be already completed at some point in the future. The usual English translation is *will have _____ed.*

> When you come into the room, I will have finished my project.

In this sentence, *I will have finished* will be completed when the action *you come* occurs in the future.

Here is the formula for the future perfect tense:

> Perfect active system root + Future (almost) of **sum** = Future perfect tense

The only difference in form from the future tense of **sum** is in the third person plural, where the future perfect tense uses **-erint** instead of **-erunt**. The conjugation of every verb, including irregular verbs, is the same in the future perfect tense. Here are example charts of the future perfect tense for each conjugation:

First conjugation

amō, amāre, amāvī, amātum *love*
PERFECT ACTIVE SYSTEM ROOT amāv-

	SINGULAR		PLURAL	
FIRST PERSON	amāverō	*I will have loved*	amāverimus	*we will have loved*
SECOND PERSON	amāveris	*you will have loved*	amāveritis	*you will have loved*
THIRD PERSON	amāverit	*he/she/it will have loved*	amāverint	*they will have loved*

Second conjugation

habeō, habēre, habuī, habitum *have*
PERFECT ACTIVE SYSTEM ROOT   **habu-**

	SINGULAR		PLURAL	
FIRST PERSON	habu**erō**	*I will have had*	habu**erimus**	*we will have had*
SECOND PERSON	habu**eris**	*you will have had*	habu**eritis**	*you will have had*
THIRD PERSON	habu**erit**	*he/she/it will have had*	habu**erint**	*they will have had*

Third conjugation

agō, agere, ēgī, actum *drive, act*
PERFECT ACTIVE SYSTEM ROOT   **ēg-**

	SINGULAR		PLURAL	
FIRST PERSON	**ēgerō**	*I will have driven*	**ēgerimus**	*we will have driven*
SECOND PERSON	**ēgeris**	*you will have driven*	**ēgeritis**	*you will have driven*
THIRD PERSON	**ēgerit**	*he/she/it will have driven*	**ēgerint**	*they will have driven*

Third -**iō** conjugation

capiō, capere, cēpī, captum *take*
PERFECT ACTIVE SYSTEM ROOT   **cēp-**

	SINGULAR		PLURAL	
FIRST PERSON	cēp**erō**	*I will have taken*	cēp**erimus**	*we will have taken*
SECOND PERSON	cēp**eris**	*you will have taken*	cēp**eritis**	*you will have taken*
THIRD PERSON	cēp**erit**	*he/she/it will have taken*	cēp**erint**	*they will have taken*

Fourth conjugation

audiō, audīre, audīvī, audītum *hear*
PERFECT ACTIVE SYSTEM ROOT   **audīv-**

	SINGULAR		PLURAL	
FIRST PERSON	audīv**erō**	*I will have heard*	audīv**erimus**	*we will have heard*
SECOND PERSON	audīv**eris**	*you will have heard*	audīv**eritis**	*you will have heard*
THIRD PERSON	audīv**erit**	*he/she/it will have heard*	audīv**erint**	*they will have heard*

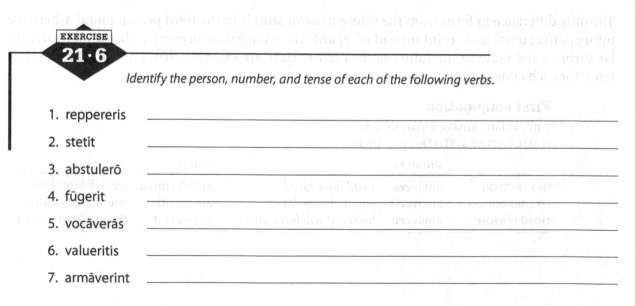

EXERCISE

21·6

Identify the person, number, and tense of each of the following verbs.

1. reppereris _____

2. stetit _____

3. abstulerō _____

4. fūgerit _____

5. vocāverās _____

6. valueritis _____

7. armāverint _____

8. surrexistī _____

9. crēdiderimus _____

10. constituerātis _____

Give the correct form of each of the following verbs.

1. prōdō (*3 sg. future perfect*) _____

2. careō (*1 pl. present*) _____

3. excipiō (*3 pl. pluperfect*) _____

4. memorō (*1 sg. imperfect*) _____

5. quiescō (*3 pl. future perfect*) _____

6. dūcō (*3 sg. future perfect*) _____

7. mandō (*2 pl. future*) _____

8. relinquō (*3 sg. imperfect*) _____

9. praestō (*2 sg. future perfect*) _____

10. percutiō (*3 pl. perfect*) _____

Keeping the same person and number, transform each of the following future-tense verbs to the future perfect.

1. ōrābunt _____

2. conficiēs _____

3. iacēbitis _____

4. dīliget _____

5. laudābis _____

6. sentiēmus _____

7. pariam _____

8. celebrābimus _____

9. instituent _____

10. habēbit _____

Translate each of the following verbs into English.

1. recesserit _____

2. fīgēbat _____

3. nescīverō _____

4. rīserant _____

5. scrībent _____

6. labōrābunt _____

7. ostendis _____

8. ignōrāverint _____

9. interficit _____

10. auxerimus _____

Translate each of the following verb phrases into Latin.

1. I had given _____

2. you (*sg.*) will have received _____

3. she has conquered _____

4. they spared _____

5. we will have closed _____

6. they will have made a sound _____

7. she had been idle _____

8. they were playing _____

9. it encircled _____

10. you (*pl.*) will free _____

Demonstrative pronouns  **·22·**

Hic haec hoc and ille illa illud

A demonstrative pronoun, like other pronouns, is used to refer to another noun. But the demonstratives also give information about the location of what is being talked about: **hic haec hoc** marks the thing being talked about as close to the speaker, while **ille illa illud** marks it as far from the speaker.

Hoc audīvistis?	*Did you hear this?*
Numquam vīdī **illum**.	*I never saw that [man].*

Here are the declensions of **hic haec hoc** and **ille illa illud**. Some of the endings will be familiar to you from nouns and adjectives you have studied.

Hic haec hoc

NUMBER	CASE	MASCULINE	FEMININE	NEUTER
SINGULAR	NOMINATIVE	hic	haec	hoc
	GENITIVE	huius	huius	huius
	DATIVE	huic	huic	huic
	ACCUSATIVE	hunc	hanc	hoc
	ABLATIVE	hōc	hāc	hōc
PLURAL	NOMINATIVE	hī	hae	haec
	GENITIVE	hōrum	hārum	hōrum
	DATIVE	hīs	hīs	hīs
	ACCUSATIVE	hōs	hās	haec
	ABLATIVE	hīs	hīs	hīs

Ille illa illud

NUMBER	CASE	MASCULINE	FEMININE	NEUTER
SINGULAR	NOMINATIVE	ille	illa	illud
	GENITIVE	illīus	illīus	illīus
	DATIVE	illī	illī	illī
	ACCUSATIVE	illum	illam	illud
	ABLATIVE	illō	illā	illō
PLURAL	NOMINATIVE	illī	illae	illa
	GENITIVE	illōrum	illārum	illōrum
	DATIVE	illīs	illīs	illīs
	ACCUSATIVE	illōs	illās	illa
	ABLATIVE	illīs	illīs	illīs

Give the correct form of each of the following pronouns.

1. hic haec hoc (*nom. sg. m.*) _____

2. ille illa illud (*acc. pl. n.*) _____

3. hic haec hoc (*gen. sg. f.*) _____

4. ille illa illud (*nom. pl. f.*) _____

5. ille illa illud (*acc. sg. m.*) _____

6. hic haec hoc (*abl. pl. f.*) _____

7. ille illa illud (*nom. sg. f.*) _____

8. hic haec hoc (*dat. sg. m.*) _____

9. hic haec hoc (*gen. pl. n.*) _____

10. hic haec hoc (*acc. sg. m.*) _____

Both of these pronouns may also act as demonstrative adjectives, modifying nouns. In this function, they have the same case, number, and gender as the noun.

Hoc verbum audīvistis?	*Did you hear this word?*
Numquam vīdī **illum** virum.	*I never saw that man.*

Translate each of the following phrases into English. Don't worry about translating the meaning of the cases.

1. hoc fātum _____

2. hōs animōs _____

3. illīs coloribus _____

4. hanc faciēm _____

5. illud caput _____

6. illae rēs _____

7. illā herbā _____

8. haec vincula _____

9. huic dominae _____

10. illārum manuum _____

Is ea id

Is ea id is a weakly demonstrative pronoun that is primarily used as a substitute for the missing third-person personal pronoun. (**Hic haec hoc** and **ille illa illud** are occasionally used in this fashion.) **Is ea id** may also function as a demonstrative adjective.

NUMBER	CASE	MASCULINE	FEMININE	NEUTER
SINGULAR	NOMINATIVE	is	ea	id
	GENITIVE	eius	eius	eius
	DATIVE	eī	eī	eī
	ACCUSATIVE	eum	eam	id
	ABLATIVE	eō	eā	eō
PLURAL	NOMINATIVE	eī	eae	ea
	GENITIVE	eōrum	eārum	eōrum
	DATIVE	eīs	eīs	eīs
	ACCUSATIVE	eōs	eās	ea
	ABLATIVE	eīs	eīs	eīs

Here are examples of the use of **is ea id**:

Is fēcit.	*He did [it].*
Ornābō **eōs** flōribus.	*I will decorate them with flowers.*
Id corpus sustulērunt.	*They lifted the/that body.*

EXERCISE
22·3

Give the form of the demonstrative adjective in parentheses that agrees with each of the following nouns. Some demonstrative adjectives may have more than one form.

1. (hic) ovēs _____

2. (is) vīs _____

3. (ille) vultū _____

4. (hic) omnia _____

5. (ille) itineribus _____

6. (is) tempore _____

7. (hic) ordinis _____

8. (ille) arbōrum _____

9. (hic) pretiō _____

10. (is) diērum _____

Translate each of the following phrases into Latin.

1. this huge number (*nom.*) _____

2. the Roman streets (*dat.*) _____

3. that lowest goddess (*acc.*) _____

4. these mortal kingdoms (*abl.*) _____

5. that lofty light (*gen.*) _____

6. the similar beginning (*nom.*) _____

7. the old priest (*acc.*) _____

8. this blind eye (*gen.*) _____

9. that sharp point (*abl.*) _____

10. the foul iron (*acc.*) _____

Reflexive pronouns and adjectives

Reflexive pronouns

A reflexive pronoun takes the place of the subject when it is referred to again in a sentence. By definition, it can only refer to the subject.

> He could hardly recognize *himself* in the mirror.
> They were getting *themselves* into trouble.

If the subject is in the third person, the reflexive pronoun has the following forms:

NUMBER	CASE	MASCULINE/ FEMININE/ NEUTER
SINGULAR	NOMINATIVE	—
	GENITIVE	suī
	DATIVE	sibi
	ACCUSATIVE	sē
	ABLATIVE	sē
PLURAL	NOMINATIVE	—
	GENITIVE	suī
	DATIVE	sibi
	ACCUSATIVE	sē
	ABLATIVE	sē

There is no nominative form, because the reflexive pronoun can only refer to an already mentioned subject. Note that the singular and plural forms are identical.

Hominēs semper **sē** amant.	*People always love themselves.*
Quisque **sibi** dedit optimum dōnum.	*Each one gave himself the best gift.*

If the subject is in the first or second person, the reflexive pronoun is the same as the personal pronoun.

Eum ad **tē** revocās?	*Are you calling him back to yourself?*
Mēcum omnia portō.	*I am carrying everything with myself.*

Reflexive adjectives

Each reflexive pronoun has a corresponding adjective that expresses possession. In the first and second persons, these are the same as the personal possessive adjectives. In the third person, both singular and plural, the reflexive possessive adjective is **suus -a -um**.

PRONOUN	POSSESSIVE/REFLEXIVE ADJECTIVE
ego	meus -a -um
nos	noster nostra nostrum
tū	tuus -a -um
vōs	vester vestra vestrum
suī	suus -a -um

Because the adjective is reflexive, it can only refer to the subject that possesses something. As an adjective, it shares the same case, number, and gender as the noun it modifies—which are not necessarily the same as those of the subject it refers back to.

EXERCISE 23·1

Translate each of the following sentences into English.

1. Augustus sibi imperātōrem sumpsit.

   _____

2. In nāvēs sē suaque conferēbant.

   _____

3. Saepe mē interrogō: "quid fēcistī?"

   _____

4. Hī amīcī certābant inter sē.

   _____

5. Amor iuvenēs ad sē properāre iussit.

   _____

6. Mox veniet cum servō suō.

   _____

7. Gallī suōs mūrōs auxērunt.

   _____

8. Pater lapidem in rogō filiī suī posuit.

   _____

9. Bene tē docēs.

   _____

10. Suōs fīnēs nōn potuit scīre.

   _____

Relative clauses

A relative clause is a complete sentence that is embedded in and linked to a larger sentence. The relative clause acts as an adjective.

> I do not like the boy *whom I saw yesterday.*
> Did you hear the stories *that were being told about you*?

Such a clause is called *relative* because of the relative pronoun, which relates the clause to a noun in the larger sentence. This noun is called the *antecedent*. The relative pronoun must have the same number and gender as its antecedent. Its case, however, is determined by its function within the relative clause.

EXERCISE
24·1

Identify the relative pronoun and its antecedent in each of the following sentences, then identify the case that the relative pronoun would use with its Latin clause.

1. The girls whom you saw ran down the street.

   _____

2. The girls who saw you ran down the street.

   _____

3. You dropped all the gifts that I had given you.

   _____

4. Look at all the colors that are in the sky!

   _____

5. Which is the one to whom you gave so much money?

   _____

6. That which she said is disgusting.

   _____

7. I lost everything that I had hidden away in the cellar.

   _____

8. They can't find the tools with which they were building the ramp.

_____

9. He still didn't know the man who was responsible.

_____

10. They told him the name of the city in which his parents lived.

_____

The relative pronoun **quī quae quod**

Following is the declension of the relative pronoun. Some of the forms are similar to those of the demonstrative pronouns.

NUMBER	CASE	MASCULINE	FEMININE	NEUTER
SINGULAR	NOMINATIVE	quī	quae	quod
	GENITIVE	cuius	cuius	cuius
	DATIVE	cui	cui	cui
	ACCUSATIVE	quem	quam	quod
	ABLATIVE	quō	quā	quō
PLURAL	NOMINATIVE	quī	quae	quae
	GENITIVE	quōrum	quārum	quōrum
	DATIVE	quibus	quibus	quibus
	ACCUSATIVE	quōs	quās	quae
	ABLATIVE	quibus	quibus	quibus

EXERCISE

24·2

Give the correct form of the relative pronoun in each of the following sentences, then translate the sentence into English.

1. Edimus fructūs _____ terra gignit.

_____

2. Optō audīre id _____ dē mē cogitābat.

_____

3. Canēs tandem agmina _____ custōdēs sunt invēnerant.

_____

4. Ecce Rōma, _____ est caput mundī.

_____

5. Ille erat vir _____ tālēs fābulās scripsit.

_____

6. Ēvādimus haec tēla, _____ adversī nōs occīdere volunt.

_____

7. Laudāvimus hominēs _____ bona faciunt.

_____

8. Ea, _____ probat populus, nesciō.

_____

9. Nāvēs in _____ nōs sumus percutiēbant ventī.

_____

10. Dīvum Phoebum, _____ frāter Iuppiter est, nimis timent.

_____

 **·25·** # Voice • The passive voice • The present passive tense

Voice

Voice is one of the characteristics of Latin verbs. A verb's voice indicates the relationship of the nominative case to the verb.

- ♦ If the voice is active, the nominative case marks the doer of the verb's action.

- ♦ If the voice is passive, the nominative case marks the receiver of the verb's action.

All of the verb forms you've studied so far have been active. A passive verb is formed like an active verb: personal endings provide information about the person and number of the subject. But Latin marks verbs in the passive voice by attaching a different set of personal endings than the ones you already know. Here are the passive personal endings:

	SINGULAR	PLURAL
FIRST PERSON	-r	-mur
SECOND PERSON	-ris	-minī
THIRD PERSON	-tur	-ntur

The present passive tense

Forming the present passive is as simple as swapping the active personal endings for the passive ones. The usual English translation is *is _____ed* or *is being _____ed*. Here is the formula for the present passive tense:

Present system root + Passive personal endings = Present passive

On the following page are example charts of the present passive tense for each conjugation.

First conjugation

amō, amāre, amāvī, amātum *love*
PRESENT SYSTEM ROOT   amā-

	SINGULAR		PLURAL	
FIRST PERSON	amor	*I am loved*	amāmur	*we are loved*
SECOND PERSON	amāris	*you are loved*	amāminī	*you are loved*
THIRD PERSON	amātur	*he/she/it is loved*	amantur	*they are loved*

Second conjugation

teneō, tenēre, tenuī, tentum *hold*
PRESENT SYSTEM ROOT   tenē-

	SINGULAR		PLURAL	
FIRST PERSON	teneor	*I am held*	tenēmur	*we are held*
SECOND PERSON	tenēris	*you are held*	tenēminī	*you are held*
THIRD PERSON	tenētur	*he/she/it is held*	tenentur	*they are held*

Third conjugation

pōnō, pōnere, posuī, positum *put*
PRESENT SYSTEM ROOT   pōne-

	SINGULAR		PLURAL	
FIRST PERSON	pōnor	*I am put*	pōnimur	*we are put*
SECOND PERSON	pōneris*	*you are put*	pōniminī	*you are put*
THIRD PERSON	pōnitur	*he/she/it is put*	pōnuntur	*they are put*

Third -iō conjugation

capiō, capere, cēpī, captum *take*
PRESENT SYSTEM ROOT   cape-

	SINGULAR		PLURAL	
FIRST PERSON	capior	*I am taken*	capimur	*we are taken*
SECOND PERSON	caperis*	*you are taken*	capiminī	*you are taken*
THIRD PERSON	capitur	*he/she/it is taken*	capiuntur	*they are taken*

Fourth conjugation

audiō, audīre, audīvī, audītum *hear*
PRESENT SYSTEM ROOT   audī-

	SINGULAR		PLURAL	
FIRST PERSON	audior	*I am heard*	audīmur	*we are heard*
SECOND PERSON	audīris	*you are heard*	audīminī	*you are heard*
THIRD PERSON	audītur	*he/she/it is heard*	audiuntur	*they are heard*

---

*Notice the unexpected -**e**- in the second person singular of the third and third -**iō** conjugations.

Give the correct form of each of the following verbs.

1. doceō (*2 sg. present passive*) _____

2. fingō (*3 sg. present passive*) _____

3. cūrō (*2 pl. present passive*) _____

4. compōnō (*3 pl. present passive*) _____

5. retineō (*1 sg. present passive*) _____

6. dēcipiō (*3 sg. present passive*) _____

7. neglegō (*1 pl. present passive*) _____

8. bibō (*3 pl. present passive*) _____

9. moneō (*3 sg. present passive*) _____

10. nōminō (*2 sg. present passive*) _____

Keeping the same person and number, transform each of the following active-voice verbs to the passive voice.

1. sepelit _____

2. requirō _____

3. petunt _____

4. videt _____

5. vocāmus _____

6. condis _____

7. rumpunt _____

8. ornātis _____

9. vincit _____

10. narrant _____

Translate each of the following verbs into English.

1. scriberis _____

2. iubētur _____

3. mittuntur _____

4. probāminī _____

5. adduntur _____

6. tangor _____

7. funditur _____

8. tolleris _____

9. moventur _____

10. spargimur _____

The ablative of personal agent

Because the passive voice effectively removes the doer of the verb's action—the nominative case marks the receiver of the action, not the doer—Latin uses a different construction to indicate whom the action is performed by. This construction is called the *ablative of personal agent*. The doer of the action is in the ablative after the preposition **ab/ā**.

Ea **ab Augustō** amātur.	*She is loved by Augustus.*
Ego **ā dominō** vocor.	*I am being called by my master.*

This construction applies only to agents that are people. If the action is performed by an inanimate object, then the ablative of means is used instead.

EXERCISE 25·4

Translate each of the following sentences into English.

1. Cūr tanta praemia mihi dantur?

_____

2. Cunctus ordō in urbe confertur.

_____

3. Diēs dīvīditur in duās partēs.

_____

4. Id nunc ā mē committitur dubiīs aurīs.

_____

5. Ā magistrō meō pecūnia nōn accipitur.

_____

6. Premimur saeculō gravī.

_____

7. In fīnibus huius urbis ā populō rēs reguntur.

_____

8. Saevae aquae hīs ripīs continentur.

_____

9. Nōs ā nostrīs amīcīs exspectāmur.

_____

10. Exercitus ā duce armātur.

_____

·26·

The imperfect and future passive tenses

Both the imperfect and future tenses of the passive voice are formed in the same way as the present tense passive: passive personal endings are substituted for active personal endings. Other than this, the passive formation is almost identical to that of the active voice.

The imperfect passive tense

The imperfect passive expresses the same idea as the imperfect active, of ongoing or repeated action in the past. The usual English translation is *was being _____ed*. Here is the formula for the imperfect passive tense:

Present system root + **-bā-** + Passive personal endings = Imperfect passive

On the following page are example charts of the imperfect passive tense for each conjugation.

First conjugation

amō, amāre, amāvī, amātum *love*

PRESENT SYSTEM ROOT **amā-**

	SINGULAR		PLURAL	
FIRST PERSON	amā**bar**	*I was being loved*	amā**bā**mur	*we were being loved*
SECOND PERSON	amā**bā**ris	*you were being loved*	amā**bā**minī	*you were being loved*
THIRD PERSON	amā**bā**tur	*he/she/it was being loved*	amā**ban**tur	*they were being loved*

Second conjugation

teneō, tenēre, tenuī, tentum *hold*

PRESENT SYSTEM ROOT **tenē-**

	SINGULAR		PLURAL	
FIRST PERSON	tenē**bar**	*I was being held*	tenē**bā**mur	*we were being held*
SECOND PERSON	tenē**bā**ris	*you were being held*	tenē**bā**minī	*you were being held*
THIRD PERSON	tenē**bā**tur	*he/she/it was being held*	tenē**ban**tur	*they were being held*

Third conjugation

pōnō, pōnere, posuī, positum *put*

PRESENT SYSTEM ROOT **pōne-**

	SINGULAR		PLURAL	
FIRST PERSON	pōnē**bar**	*I was being put*	pōnē**bā**mur	*we were being put*
SECOND PERSON	pōnē**bā**ris	*you were being put*	pōnē**bā**minī	*you were being put*
THIRD PERSON	pōnē**bā**tur	*he/she/it was being put*	pōnē**ban**tur	*they were being put*

Third -iō conjugation

capiō, capere, cēpī, captum *take*

PRESENT SYSTEM ROOT **cape-**

	SINGULAR		PLURAL	
FIRST PERSON	capiē**bar**	*I was being taken*	capiē**bā**mur	*we were being taken*
SECOND PERSON	capiē**bā**ris	*you were being taken*	capiē**bā**minī	*you were being taken*
THIRD PERSON	capiē**bā**tur	*he/she/it was being taken*	capiē**ban**tur	*they were being taken*

Fourth conjugation

audiō, audīre, audīvī, audītum *hear*

PRESENT SYSTEM ROOT **audī-**

	SINGULAR		PLURAL	
FIRST PERSON	audiē**bar**	*I was being heard*	audiē**bā**mur	*we were being heard*
SECOND PERSON	audiē**bā**ris	*you were being heard*	audiē**bā**minī	*you were being heard*
THIRD PERSON	audiē**bā**tur	*he/she/it was being heard*	audiē**ban**tur	*they were being heard*

Identify the person, number, and tense of each of the following verbs, then translate the verb into English.

1. appellantur _____

2. dīligor _____

3. ducēbāris _____

4. relinquēbātur _____

5. datur _____

6. creābantur _____

7. geritur _____

8. habēbāminī _____

9. prōmittēbāmur _____

10. dēferēbātur _____

Give the correct form of each of the following verbs.

1. trahō (*2 sg. present passive*) _____

2. vertō (*3 pl. imperfect passive*) _____

3. dīcō (*3 sg. present passive*) _____

4. portō (*1 pl. imperfect passive*) _____

5. ōrō (*2 sg. imperfect passive*) _____

6. audiō (*3 pl. imperfect passive*) _____

7. vehō (*3 sg. imperfect passive*) _____

8. prōpōnō (*3 pl. present passive*) _____

9. parō (*1 sg. imperfect passive*) _____

10. cingō (*3 sg. imperfect passive*) _____

Translate each of the following verb phrases into Latin.

1. I was being snatched _____

2. he was being brought _____

3. they are collected _____

4. it was being discovered _____

5. we are being established _____

6. she is predicted _____

7. you (*pl.*) are recognized _____

8. they were being eaten _____

9. you (*sg.*) were being taken up _____

10. he is perceived _____

The future passive tense

The future passive is usually translated into English as *will be _____ed*. Here is the formula for the future passive:

Present system root + -**b**-/-**bi**-/-**bu**- or -**a**-/-**ē**- + Passive personal endings = Future passive

Just as in the active voice, the first and second conjugations use the -**b**- markers for the future, while the third, third -**iō**, and fourth conjugations use -**ē**- as a tense marker. This distinction is important; otherwise, it's difficult to tell a second-conjugation present tense from a third-conjugation future tense.

Here are example charts of the future passive tense for each conjugation:

First conjugation

amō, amāre, amāvī, amātum *love*
PRESENT SYSTEM ROOT   amā-

	SINGULAR		PLURAL	
FIRST PERSON	amā**bor**	*I will be loved*	amā**bimur**	*we will be loved*
SECOND PERSON	amā**beris***	*you will be loved*	amā**biminī**	*you will be loved*
THIRD PERSON	amā**bitur**	*he/she/it will be loved*	amā**buntur**	*they will be loved*

Second conjugation

teneō, tenēre, tenuī, tentum *hold*
PRESENT SYSTEM ROOT   tenē-

	SINGULAR		PLURAL	
FIRST PERSON	tenē**bor**	*I will be held*	tenē**bimur**	*we will be held*
SECOND PERSON	tenē**beris***	*you will be held*	tenē**biminī**	*you will be held*
THIRD PERSON	tenē**bitur**	*he/she/it will be held*	tenē**buntur**	*they will be held*

*Notice the unexpected -**e**- in the second person singular of the first and second conjugations.

Third conjugation

pōnō, pōnere, posuī, positum *put*
PRESENT SYSTEM ROOT   pōne-

	SINGULAR		PLURAL	
FIRST PERSON	pōnar	*I will be put*	pōnēmur	*we will be put*
SECOND PERSON	pōnēris	*you will be put*	pōnēminī	*you will be put*
THIRD PERSON	pōnētur	*he/she/it will be put*	pōnentur	*they will be put*

Third -iō conjugation

capiō, capere, cēpī, captum *take*
PRESENT SYSTEM ROOT   cape-

	SINGULAR		PLURAL	
FIRST PERSON	capiar	*I will be taken*	capiēmur	*we will be taken*
SECOND PERSON	capiēris	*you will be taken*	capiēminī	*you will be taken*
THIRD PERSON	capiētur	*he/she/it will be taken*	capientur	*they will be taken*

Fourth conjugation

audiō, audīre, audīvī, audītum *hear*
PRESENT SYSTEM ROOT   audī-

	SINGULAR		PLURAL	
FIRST PERSON	audiar	*I will be heard*	audiēmur	*we will be heard*
SECOND PERSON	audiēris	*you will be heard*	audiēminī	*you will be heard*
THIRD PERSON	audiētur	*he/she/it will be heard*	audientur	*they will be heard*

EXERCISE 26·4

Identify the person, number, and tense of each of the following verbs, then translate the verb into English.

1. recipientur _____

2. discēbātur _____

3. instituimur _____

4. metuētur _____

5. ascendētur _____

6. suscipiēminī _____

7. claudēbantur _____

8. miscēbitur _____

9. ēripiar _____

10. regnātur _____

26·5

Give the correct form of each of the following verbs.

1. revocō (*2 sg. present passive*) _____

2. dīrigō (*3 pl. imperfect passive*) _____

3. praebeō (*1 sg. future passive*) _____

4. existimō (*3 pl. present passive*) _____

5. convertō (*3 pl. future passive*) _____

6. impleō (*3 sg. future passive*) _____

7. cōgō (*1 pl. imperfect passive*) _____

8. cupiō (*3 pl. future passive*) _____

9. ignōrō (*3 sg. future passive*) _____

10. contemnō (*2 pl. future passive*) _____

EXERCISE

26·6

Translate each of the following verb phrases into Latin.

1. he will be joined _____

2. it was being shown _____

3. they are being saved _____

4. we will be worshipped _____

5. I will be harmed _____

6. it will be increased _____

7. you (*pl.*) were being handed over _____

8. they are being lost _____

9. he will be broken _____

10. you (*sg.*) will be praised _____

 **·27· The perfect passive tense**

The perfect passive expresses either of the same two meanings as the perfect active, but from the passive perspective:

1. An action performed instantaneously in the past (the simple perfect)
2. An action performed in the past and completed as of right now (the present perfect)

The usual English translation is *was _____ed* or *has been _____ed.*

The perfect passive is built in a different way than the other verb forms you've seen so far, because it is constructed from two separate words. The first word comes from the perfect passive root—the fourth principal part, also called the perfect passive participle. This first word is treated like an **-us -a -um** adjective modifying the subject, and so it must have the same number and gender as the subject. The second word is a form of the present tense of **sum**.

Puell**a** am**āta** est.	*The girl was loved.*
Ciner**ēs** str**ātī** sunt.	*The ashes have been strewn.*

The conjugation of every verb, including irregular verbs, is the same in the perfect passive tense. Here is the formula for the perfect passive:

Perfect passive system root + Present tense of **sum** = Perfect passive

On the following page are example charts of the perfect passive tense for each conjugation. To illustrate how the first part of the verb form must agree with the subject, the charts assume subjects of different genders.

First conjugation

amō, amāre, amāvī, amātum *love*
PERFECT PASSIVE SYSTEM ROOT amāt-
GENDER OF SUBJECT Masculine

	SINGULAR		PLURAL	
FIRST PERSON	amātus sum	*I was loved*	amātī sumus	*we were loved*
SECOND PERSON	amātus es	*you were loved*	amātī estis	*you were loved*
THIRD PERSON	amātus est	*he was loved*	amātī sunt	*they were loved*

Second conjugation

teneō, tenēre, tenuī, tentum *hold*
PERFECT PASSIVE SYSTEM ROOT tent-
GENDER OF SUBJECT Masculine

	SINGULAR		PLURAL	
FIRST PERSON	tentus sum	*I was held*	tentī sumus	*we were held*
SECOND PERSON	tentus es	*you were held*	tentī estis	*you were held*
THIRD PERSON	tentus est	*he was held*	tentī sunt	*they were held*

Third conjugation

pōnō, pōnere, posuī, positum *put*
PERFECT PASSIVE SYSTEM ROOT posit-
GENDER OF SUBJECT Feminine

	SINGULAR		PLURAL	
FIRST PERSON	posita sum	*I was put*	positae sumus	*we were put*
SECOND PERSON	posita es	*you were put*	positae estis	*you were put*
THIRD PERSON	posita est	*she was put*	positae sunt	*they were put*

Third -iō conjugation

capiō, capere, cēpī, captum *take*
PERFECT PASSIVE SYSTEM ROOT capt-
GENDER OF SUBJECT Neuter

	SINGULAR		PLURAL	
FIRST PERSON	captum sum	*I was taken*	capta sumus	*we were taken*
SECOND PERSON	captum es	*you were taken*	capta estis	*you were taken*
THIRD PERSON	captum est	*it was taken*	capta sunt	*they were taken*

Fourth conjugation

audiō, audīre, audīvī, audītum *hear*
PERFECT PASSIVE SYSTEM ROOT audīt-
GENDER OF SUBJECT Masculine

	SINGULAR		PLURAL	
FIRST PERSON	audītus sum	*I was heard*	audītī sumus	*we were heard*
SECOND PERSON	audītus es	*you were heard*	audītī estis	*you were heard*
THIRD PERSON	audītus est	*he was heard*	audītī sunt	*they were heard*

Identify the person, number, tense, and voice of each of the following verbs, then translate the verb into English.

1. putātus est _____

2. captum es _____

3. solvētur _____

4. genita sunt _____

5. effectum est _____

6. repertī sunt _____

7. optāvērunt _____

8. nōtae sumus _____

9. aspecta est _____

10. mōvēbāmur _____

Give the correct form of each of the following verbs. Assume a feminine subject for each.

1. conferō (*3 pl. perfect passive*) _____

2. dō (*1 sg. future passive*) _____

3. perdō (*3 sg. perfect passive*) _____

4. aperiō (*1 pl. perfect passive*) _____

5. claudō (*2 sg. perfect passive*) _____

6. cōgō (*3 pl. imperfect passive*) _____

7. intellegō (*3 pl. perfect passive*) _____

8. audiō (*3 sg. perfect passive*) _____

9. dēdūcō (*2 pl. imperfect passive*) _____

10. sūmō (*3 pl. perfect passive*) _____

Keeping the same person and number, transform each of the following perfect active verbs to perfect passives. Assume a masculine subject for each.

1. dīmīsistī   _____

2. revertit   _____

3. coluimus   _____

4. indicāvistis   _____

5. mandāvērunt   _____

6. fēcī   _____

7. cecinērunt   _____

8. lēgit   _____

9. imposuistī   _____

10. contiguit   _____

Give the perfect passive form of the verb in parentheses that agrees with each of the following subjects.

1. Omnia _____ (agō).

2. Sacerdōs _____ (quaerō).

3. Cinis _____ (pendō).

4. Dōnum _____ (dōnō).

5. Nōs (m.) _____ (interrogō).

6. Flōrēs _____ (sternō).

7. Tēlum _____ (iaciō).

8. Tū (f.) _____ (temptō).

9. Piscis _____ (teneō).

10. Vestis _____ (mereō).

Translate each of the following verb phrases into Latin.

1. you (*m. sg.*) have been created _____

2. we were being freed _____

3. I (*m.*) have been ordered _____

4. she was pursued _____

5. it was spread _____

6. he is being saved _____

7. he was thought _____

8. you (*m. pl.*) were being returned _____

9. they will be put on _____

10. I am being received _____

The pluperfect passive and future perfect passive tenses • Deponent verbs

28

The pluperfect passive and future perfect passive are built in the same way as the perfect passive. They are composed of two words, and they use the same perfect passive system root (the fourth principal part), but they use different tenses of **sum**.

The pluperfect passive tense

The pluperfect expresses completed action in the past. The usual English translation is *had been _____ed*. The conjugation of every verb, including irregular verbs, is the same in the pluperfect passive tense. Here is the formula:

Perfect passive system root + Imperfect tense of **sum** = Pluperfect passive

On the following page are example charts of the pluperfect passive tense for each conjugation. To illustrate how the first part of the verb form must agree with the subject, the charts assume subjects of different genders.

First conjugation

amō, amāre, amāvī, amātum *love*
PERFECT PASSIVE SYSTEM ROOT   amāt-
GENDER OF SUBJECT   Feminine

	SINGULAR		PLURAL	
FIRST PERSON	amāta eram	*I had been loved*	amātae erāmus	*we had been loved*
SECOND PERSON	amāta erās	*you had been loved*	amātae erātis	*you had been loved*
THIRD PERSON	amāta erat	*she had been loved*	amātae erant	*they had been loved*

Second conjugation

teneō, tenēre, tenuī, tentum *hold*
PERFECT PASSIVE SYSTEM ROOT   tent-
GENDER OF SUBJECT   Neuter

	SINGULAR		PLURAL	
FIRST PERSON	tentum eram	*I had been held*	tenta erāmus	*we had been held*
SECOND PERSON	tentum erās	*you had been held*	tenta erātis	*you had been held*
THIRD PERSON	tentum erat	*it had been held*	tenta erant	*they had been held*

Third conjugation

pōnō, pōnere, posuī, positum *put*
PERFECT PASSIVE SYSTEM ROOT   posit-
GENDER OF SUBJECT   Masculine

	SINGULAR		PLURAL	
FIRST PERSON	positus eram	*I had been put*	positī erāmus	*we had been put*
SECOND PERSON	positus erās	*you had been put*	positī erātis	*you had been put*
THIRD PERSON	positus erat	*he had been put*	positī erant	*they had been put*

Third -iō conjugation

capiō, capere, cēpī, captum *take*
PERFECT PASSIVE SYSTEM ROOT   capt-
GENDER OF SUBJECT   Masculine

	SINGULAR		PLURAL	
FIRST PERSON	captus eram	*I had been taken*	captī erāmus	*we had been taken*
SECOND PERSON	captus erās	*you had been taken*	captī erātis	*you had been taken*
THIRD PERSON	captus erat	*he had been taken*	captī erant	*they had been taken*

Fourth conjugation

audiō, audīre, audīvī, audītum *hear*
PERFECT PASSIVE SYSTEM ROOT   audīt-
GENDER OF SUBJECT   Neuter

	SINGULAR		PLURAL	
FIRST PERSON	audītum eram	*I had been heard*	audīta erāmus	*we had been heard*
SECOND PERSON	audītum erās	*you had been heard*	audīta erātis	*you had been heard*
THIRD PERSON	audītum erat	*it had been heard*	audīta erant	*they had been heard*

Identify the person, number, and tense of each of the following verbs, then translate the verb into English.

1. allātus erat _____

2. fixa erant _____

3. concessum est _____

4. neglegēbāmur _____

5. inventum erat _____

6. crēditae erātis _____

7. dīrectae sunt _____

8. impōnēris _____

9. permitteris _____

10. positī erant _____

Give the correct form of each of the following verbs. Assume a neuter subject for each.

1. trādō (*3 pl. pluperfect passive*) _____

2. āmittō (*1 sg. future passive*) _____

3. aspiciō (*1 pl. pluperfect passive*) _____

4. incipiō (*3 sg. perfect passive*) _____

5. putō (*3 pl. pluperfect passive*) _____

6. augeō (*1 pl. imperfect passive*) _____

7. requīrō (*3 pl. pluperfect passive*) _____

8. percutiō (*2 sg. pluperfect passive*) _____

9. doceō (*2 pl. pluperfect passive*) _____

10. ornō (*3 sg. perfect passive*) _____

Translate each of the following verb phrases into Latin.

1. we (*m.*) had been built _____

2. he had been dragged _____

3. you (*m. pl.*) had been ordered _____

4. she had been taught _____

5. it had been wished _____

6. they (*m.*) had been held _____

7. I (*m.*) had been conquered _____

8. he had been completed _____

9. they (*m.*) had been given as a gift _____

10. you (*m. sg.*) had been hoped _____

The future perfect passive tense

The future perfect passive expresses completed action in the future. The usual English translation is *will have been* _____ *ed*. Here is the formula:

Perfect passive system root + Future tense of **sum** = Future perfect passive

The conjugation of every verb, including irregular verbs, is the same in the future perfect passive.

On the following page are example charts of the future perfect passive tense for each conjugation. To illustrate how the first part of the verb form must agree with the subject, the charts assume subjects of different genders.

First conjugation

amō, amāre, amāvī, amātum *love*
PERFECT PASSIVE SYSTEM ROOT   amāt-
GENDER OF SUBJECT   Masculine

	SINGULAR		PLURAL	
FIRST PERSON	amātus erō	*I will have been loved*	amātī erimus	*we will have been loved*
SECOND PERSON	amātus eris	*you will have been loved*	amātī eritis	*you will have been loved*
THIRD PERSON	amātus erit	*he will have been loved*	amātī erunt	*they will have been loved*

Second conjugation

teneō, tenēre, tenuī, tentum *hold*
PERFECT PASSIVE SYSTEM ROOT   tent-
GENDER OF SUBJECT   Masculine

	SINGULAR		PLURAL	
FIRST PERSON	tentus erō	*I will have been held*	tentī erimus	*we will have been held*
SECOND PERSON	tentus eris	*you will have been held*	tentī eritis	*you will have been held*
THIRD PERSON	tentus erit	*he will have been held*	tentī erunt	*they will have been held*

Third conjugation

pōnō, pōnere, posuī, positum *put*
PERFECT PASSIVE SYSTEM ROOT   posit-
GENDER OF SUBJECT   Feminine

	SINGULAR		PLURAL	
FIRST PERSON	posita erō	*I will have been put*	positae erimus	*we will have been put*
SECOND PERSON	posita eris	*you will have been put*	positae eritis	*you will have been put*
THIRD PERSON	posita erit	*she will have been put*	positae erunt	*they will have been put*

Third -iō conjugation

capiō, capere, cēpī, captum *take*
PERFECT PASSIVE SYSTEM ROOT   capt-
GENDER OF SUBJECT   Neuter

	SINGULAR		PLURAL	
FIRST PERSON	captum erō	*I will have been taken*	capta erimus	*we will have been taken*
SECOND PERSON	captum eris	*you will have been taken*	capta eritis	*you will have been taken*
THIRD PERSON	captum erit	*it will have been taken*	capta erunt	*they will have been taken*

Fourth conjugation

audiō, audīre, audīvī, audītum *hear*
PERFECT PASSIVE SYSTEM ROOT   audīt-
GENDER OF SUBJECT   Masculine

	SINGULAR		PLURAL	
FIRST PERSON	audītus erō	*I will have been heard*	audītī erimus	*we will have been heard*
SECOND PERSON	audītus eris	*you will have been heard*	audītī eritis	*you will have been heard*
THIRD PERSON	audītus erit	*he will have been heard*	audītī erunt	*they will have been heard*

Identify the person, number, and tense of each of the following verbs, then translate the verb into English.

1. intellecta erunt _____

2. superātus erō _____

3. raptum erit _____

4. conspecta es _____

5. rectī erant _____

6. monitae erimus _____

7. relictum erit _____

8. praebitī eritis _____

9. iūtī erunt _____

10. percussa erant _____

Give the correct form of each of the following verbs. Assume a masculine subject for each.

1. accipiō (*3 pl. future perfect passive*) _____

2. audiō (*2 sg. present passive*) _____

3. tollō (*3 pl. perfect passive*) _____

4. sentiō (*3 sg. future perfect passive*) _____

5. pandō (*1 pl. future perfect passive*) _____

6. misceō (*3 sg. imperfect passive*) _____

7. faciō (*3 pl. future perfect passive*) _____

8. gerō (*2 sg. pluperfect passive*) _____

9. armō (*2 pl. future perfect passive*) _____

10. petō (*1 pl. future perfect passive*) _____

Translate each of the following verb phrases into Latin.

1. you (*m. sg.*) will have been praised _____

2. he will have been demanded _____

3. it will have been said _____

4. they (*m.*) have been touched _____

5. you (*m. pl.*) will have been entrusted _____

6. it was being turned _____

7. they (*m.*) will have been joined _____

8. she will have been led _____

9. we (*m.*) will have been compelled _____

10. he will have been sent _____

Deponent verbs

There is a small group of Latin verbs that appear only in passive forms, yet retain active meanings. These are called *deponent verbs*, and you can recognize them by the way they are listed in dictionaries.

> **cōnor, cōnārī, cōnātus** attempt
> **loquor, loquī, locūtus** speak

Any verb listed with passive forms like this is a deponent verb. Be careful: unless you realize that a verb is deponent, nothing else will alert you that it has active meanings instead of passive ones.

Translate each of the following sentences into English. Watch out for deponent verbs!

1. Ea quae requīsīta erant parāta sunt.

_____

2. Humus nōn in manūs sūmitur.

_____

3. Nihil tēcum frāter locūtus est?

_____

4. Nova templa Iovī constitūta erunt.

_____

5. Ducem, cuius sententiam semper secūtus sum, exspectābam.

_____

6. Nuntiī ab omnibus audiēbantur.

_____

7. Saepe eum cōnāmur docēre.

_____

8. Quondam hostēs nunc iunctī sunt amīcitiā.

_____

9. Vīnum fūsum erat cum exercitus Rōmānus pervēnit.

_____

10. Sōlēs oriuntur et diem ferunt.

_____

VOCABULARY

Common deponent verbs

complector, complectī, complexus	_embrace_
confiteor, confitērī, confessus	_admit_
cōnōr, cōnārī, cōnātus	_attempt_
consequor, consequī, consecūtus	_follow_
ēgredior, ēgredī, ēgressus	_exit_
experior, experīrī, expertus	_test_
imitor, imitārī, imitātus	_imitate_
ingredior, ingredī, ingressus	_enter_
īrascor, īrascī, īrātus	_get angry_
loquor, loquī, locūtus	_speak_
mīror, mīrārī, mīrātus	_be amazed_
morior, morī, mortuus	_die_
nascor, nascī, nātus	_be born_
orior, orīrī, ortus	_rise_
patior, patī, passus	_suffer_
precor, precārī, precātus	_pray_
queror, querī, questus	_complain_
sequor, sequī, secūtus	_follow_
ūtor, ūtī, ūsus	_use_

Participles

29

Participles are verbs acting as adjectives and, as a result, have a dual nature.

1. Like adjectives, they describe nouns (and agree with the nouns in case, number, and gender).
2. Like verbs, they can have direct objects and other verbal constructions.

Latin has four participles, representing both voices and three tenses. Here are their English counterparts:

To love

PRESENT ACTIVE PARTICIPLE	*loving*
PERFECT PASSIVE PARTICIPLE	*having been loved* OR *loved*
FUTURE ACTIVE PARTICIPLE	*about to love* OR *going to love*
FUTURE PASSIVE PARTICIPLE	*about to be loved* OR *going to be loved* OR *to be loved*

The present active participle

The present active participle is formed from the present system root. To that root is added **-nt-** and third-declension one-ending adjective endings. The nominative case ends in **-ns**. Here is the formula for the present active participle:

Present system root + **-nt-** + Third-declension adjective endings
= Present active participle

First conjugation

NUMBER	CASE	MASCULINE/ FEMININE	NEUTER
SINGULAR	NOMINATIVE	ama**ns**	ama**ns**
	GENITIVE	ama**ntis**	ama**ntis**
	DATIVE	ama**ntī**	ama**ntī**
	ACCUSATIVE	ama**ntem**	ama**ns**
	ABLATIVE	ama**ntī**	ama**ntī**
	VOCATIVE	ama**ns**	ama**ns**
PLURAL	NOMINATIVE	ama**ntēs**	ama**ntia**
	GENITIVE	ama**ntium**	ama**ntium**
	DATIVE	ama**ntibus**	ama**ntibus**
	ACCUSATIVE	ama**ntēs**	ama**ntia**
	ABLATIVE	ama**ntibus**	ama**ntibus**
	VOCATIVE	ama**ntēs**	ama**ntia**

Second conjugation

NUMBER	CASE	MASCULINE/FEMININE	NEUTER
SINGULAR	NOMINATIVE	tenens	tenens
	GENITIVE	tenentis	tenentis
	DATIVE	tenentī	tenentī
	ACCUSATIVE	tenentem	tenens
	ABLATIVE	tenentī	tenentī
	VOCATIVE	tenens	tenens
PLURAL	NOMINATIVE	tenentēs	tenentia
	GENITIVE	tenentium	tenentium
	DATIVE	tenentibus	tenentibus
	ACCUSATIVE	tenentēs	tenentia
	ABLATIVE	tenentibus	tenentibus
	VOCATIVE	tenentēs	tenentia

Third conjugation

NUMBER	CASE	MASCULINE/FEMININE	NEUTER
SINGULAR	NOMINATIVE	pōnens	pōnens
	GENITIVE	pōnentis	pōnentis
	DATIVE	pōnentī	pōnentī
	ACCUSATIVE	pōnentem	pōnens
	ABLATIVE	pōnentī	pōnentī
	VOCATIVE	pōnens	pōnens
PLURAL	NOMINATIVE	pōnentēs	pōnentia
	GENITIVE	pōnentium	pōnentium
	DATIVE	pōnentibus	pōnentibus
	ACCUSATIVE	pōnentēs	pōnentia
	ABLATIVE	pōnentibus	pōnentibus
	VOCATIVE	pōnentēs	pōnentia

Third -iō conjugation

NUMBER	CASE	MASCULINE/FEMININE	NEUTER
SINGULAR	NOMINATIVE	capiens	capiens
	GENITIVE	capientis	capientis
	DATIVE	capientī	capientī
	ACCUSATIVE	capientem	capiens
	ABLATIVE	capientī	capientī
	VOCATIVE	capiens	capiens
PLURAL	NOMINATIVE	capientēs	capientia
	GENITIVE	capientium	capientium
	DATIVE	capientibus	capientibus
	ACCUSATIVE	capientēs	capientia
	ABLATIVE	capientibus	capientibus
	VOCATIVE	capientēs	capientia

Fourth conjugation

NUMBER	CASE	MASCULINE/FEMININE	NEUTER
SINGULAR	NOMINATIVE	audiens	audiens
	GENITIVE	audientis	audientis
	DATIVE	audientī	audientī
	ACCUSATIVE	audientem	audiens
	ABLATIVE	audientī	audientī
	VOCATIVE	audiens	audiens
PLURAL	NOMINATIVE	audientēs	audientia
	GENITIVE	audientium	audientium
	DATIVE	audientibus	audientibus
	ACCUSATIVE	audientēs	audientia
	ABLATIVE	audientibus	audientibus
	VOCATIVE	audientēs	audientia

EXERCISE 29·1

Give the correct form of the present active participle of each of the following verbs.

1. certō (*acc. sg. m.*) _____

2. pariō (*dat. pl. f.*) _____

3. dormiō (*gen. sg. m.*) _____

4. consulō (*nom. sg. n.*) _____

5. rīdeō (*gen. pl. n.*) _____

6. careō (*dat. sg. m.*) _____

7. interficiō (*nom. pl. m.*) _____

8. peccō (*abl. pl. f.*) _____

9. surgō (*acc. sg. n.*) _____

10. tendō (*nom. sg. m.*) _____

The perfect passive participle

The perfect passive participle is formed from the perfect passive system root—in fact, it is practically the same as the fourth principal part. The perfect passive participle is an adjective in **-us -a -um** built from this root.

CONJUGATION	FOURTH PRINCIPAL PART	MASCULINE/FEMININE/NEUTER
FIRST	amātum	amātus amāta amātum
SECOND	habitum	habitus habita habitum
THIRD	actum	actus acta actum
THIRD **-iō**	captum	captus capta captum
FOURTH	audītum	audītus audīta audītum

Give the correct form of the perfect passive participle of each of the following verbs.

1. doceō (*dat. pl. m.*) _____

2. mūtō (*acc. sg. n.*) _____

3. concēdō (*gen. sg. m.*) _____

4. dēficiō (*acc. pl. n.*) _____

5. nesciō (*nom. pl. m.*) _____

6. edō (*nom. sg. m.*) _____

7. dēfendō (*abl. sg. f.*) _____

8. iūrō (*gen. sg. f.*) _____

9. occīdō (*acc. pl. n.*) _____

10. narrō (*dat. pl. m.*) _____

The future active participle

The future active participle is, surprisingly, built from the perfect passive system root. The future tense marker, **-ūr-**, is added to the root before the **-us -a -um** adjective endings.

CONJUGATION	MASCULINE/FEMININE/NEUTER
FIRST	amātūrus amātūra amātūrum
SECOND	habitūrus habitūra habitūrum
THIRD	actūrus actūra actūrum
THIRD **-iŏ**	captūrus captūra captūrum
FOURTH	audītūrus audītūra audītūrum

Give the correct form of the future active participle of each of the following verbs.

1. videō (*nom. pl. f.*) _____

2. exerceō (*gen. sg. m.*) _____

3. vehō (*acc. pl. f.*) _____

4. amō (*abl. sg. m.*) _____

5. pergō (*nom. pl. f.*) _____

6. conspiciō (*acc. sg. m.*) _____

7. fluō (*gen. pl. n.*) _____

8. rogō (*nom. sg. m.*) _____

9. cadō (*dat. pl. n.*) _____

10. dēsīderō (*acc. sg. m.*) _____

The future passive participle

The future passive participle is built from the present system root. To that root is added the tense marker **-nd-**, followed by the **-us -a -um** adjective endings.

CONJUGATION	MASCULINE/FEMININE/NEUTER
FIRST	amandus amanda amandum
SECOND	habendus habenda habendum
THIRD	agendus agenda agendum
THIRD **-iō**	capiendus capienda capiendum
FOURTH	audiendus audienda audiendum

EXERCISE 29·4

Give the correct form of the future passive participle of each of the following verbs.

1. iubeō (*abl. sg. m.*) _____

2. putō (*nom. sg. f.*) _____

3. tangō (*gen. sg. m.*) _____

4. discō (*acc. sg. m.*) _____

5. augeō (*abl. sg. f.*) _____

6. faciō (*nom. pl. n.*) _____

7. ēvādō (*acc. pl. n.*) _____

8. imperō (*dat. pl. n.*) _____

9. ēripiō (*abl. pl. f.*) _____

10. temptō (*nom. pl. m.*) _____

EXERCISE 29·5

Identify the case, number, gender, tense, and voice of each of the following participles.

1. falsīs _____

2. currentēs _____

3. discessūrī _____

4. cōgitantem _____

5. respōnsō _____

6. perditōs _____

7. tangendās _____

8. negātum _____

9. existimātūrīs _____

10. strātīs _____

Translate each of the following sentences into English.

1. Vōta virōrum armātōrum ignōrābantur.

   _____

2. Sermōnī bene prōditō laudēs datae sunt.

   _____

3. Eīs quattuor pulchrīs lēgibus hominēs intellegentēs gaudēre potuērunt.

   _____

4. Laudāmus rēgem hostēs pugnantem.

   _____

5. Haec scrībentium culpa iam contempta erat.

   _____

6. Nuntiī in partēs ignōtās missī erunt.

   _____

7. Omnēs servī, ā dominō vocātī, properābant.

   _____

8. Vir fēminaque iungendī sacerdōtem petīvērunt.

   _____

9. Ā mīlite hostibus trāditō turrēs inventae sunt.

   _____

10. Bacchum convīvium inceptūrum retinēmus.

   _____

The ablative absolute

30

The ablative absolute is an extremely compact subordinate clause that provides extra information about the circumstances of the action of the independent clause. Although it does not make the relationship explicit, it can express the following four circumstances about the independent clause:

1. Time (*when/while/after*)
2. Cause (*because*)
3. Condition (*if*)
4. Concession (*although*)

Here are some examples:

Exercitū victō, urbs tōta timet.	*Because the army was defeated, the whole city is afraid.*
Patre vī ventī, nōs tūtī sumus.	*If our father is living, we are safe.*

The ablative absolute has two essential parts:

1. A noun in the ablative
2. A modifier—most often, but not always, a participle—also in the ablative

Matre occīsā, . . .	*When my mother had been killed . . .*
Augustō imperātōre, . . .	*While Augustus is emperor . . .*

Translating the ablative absolute

To translate an ablative absolute into English, it is necessary to create a complete dependent clause out of a set of words in the ablative case. This is a simple process. The ablative noun becomes the subject of the dependent clause, and the modifier, usually a participle, becomes the verb of the clause. Then you have to decide the specific meaning of the clause (*when, because, if, although*), so that you can use the appropriate conjunction at the beginning.

Start with the ablative absolute

ABLATIVE NOUN	PARTICIPLE
litterīs	missīs
letters	*having been sent*

and change it to a dependent
clause in English

When
Because
If
Although

SUBJECT	CONJUGATED VERB
the letters	were sent, . . .

EXERCISE 30·1

Translate each of the following phrases into Latin using an ablative absolute.

1. when the sun is rising _____

2. while the guardian stays awake _____

3. if the leader is living _____

4. although the songs were sung _____

5. because the master was deceived _____

6. after the two were joined _____

7. when the food was brought in _____

8. if the sea is not calm _____

9. because the world was not known _____

10. when the moon is increasing _____

EXERCISE 30·2

Translate each of the following sentences into English.

1. Tē dormientī, Bacchus nōbīs apparuit.

_____

2. Mensā positā, omnēs virginēs conveniunt.

_____

3. Verbīs dictīs, iūdicium perfectum est.

_____

4. Victōre discessūrō, flēbit māter.

_____

5. Cīvitāte ā paucīs dēfensā, mox moenia urbis huius ascendētis.

_____

6. Marte duce, plūra corpora per viās sternuntur.

_____

7. Argentō repertō, is tamen nōn confessus est.

_____

8. Rōmā vīsā, Phoebō vōta dēbēbunt.

_____

9. Fīliō ab hostibus interfectō, victōriam tamen spērant parentēs.

_____

10. Ventīs adversīs, quō īre nāvibus precāris?

_____

Infinitives • Indirect statement

Infinitives

You have already studied the present active infinitive, which is the second principal part of a verb. The infinitive is commonly used as a subject, an object, or a complementary infinitive with verbs like **possum**. But it is only one of six Latin infinitives, which cover both voices and three tenses.

Forming the infinitives

Here are the formulas for Latin's six infinitives:

INFINITIVE	FORMATION
PRESENT ACTIVE	Second principal part
PRESENT PASSIVE	Present system root + **-rī**
PERFECT ACTIVE	Perfect active system root + **-isse**
PERFECT PASSIVE	Fourth principal part + **esse** (the infinitive of **sum**)
FUTURE ACTIVE	Future active participle + **esse**
FUTURE PASSIVE	Fourth principal part + **īrī** (the passive infinitive of **eō**)

Note that, for the present passive infinitive, the third and third **-iō** conjugations drop the vowel at the end of the root and add **-ī**.

On the following page are example charts of all the infinitives for each conjugation.

138

Present infinitives

CONJUGATION	ACTIVE INFINITIVE		PASSIVE INFINITIVE	
FIRST	amāre	*to love*	amārī	*to be loved*
SECOND	tenēre	*to hold*	tenērī	*to be held*
THIRD	pōnere	*to put*	pōnī	*to be put*
THIRD -**iŏ**	capere	*to take*	capī	*to be taken*
FOURTH	audīre	*to hear*	audīrī	*to be heard*

Perfect infinitives

CONJUGATION	ACTIVE INFINITIVE		PASSIVE INFINITIVE	
FIRST	amāvisse	*to have loved*	amātum esse	*to have been loved*
SECOND	tenuisse	*to have held*	tentum esse	*to have been held*
THIRD	posuisse	*to have put*	positum esse	*to have been put*
THIRD -**iŏ**	cēpisse	*to have taken*	captum esse	*to have been taken*
FOURTH	audīvisse	*to have heard*	audītum esse	*to have been heard*

Future infinitives

CONJUGATION	ACTIVE INFINITIVE		PASSIVE INFINITIVE	
FIRST	amātūrum esse	*to be going to love*	amātum īrī	*to be going to be loved*
SECOND	tentūrum esse	*to be going to hold*	tentum īrī	*to be going to be held*
THIRD	positūrum esse	*to be going to put*	positum īrī	*to be going to be put*
THIRD -**iŏ**	captūrum esse	*to be going to take*	captum īrī	*to be going to be taken*
FOURTH	audītūrum esse	*to be going to hear*	audītum īrī	*to be going to be heard*

The infinitives of sum

The irregular verb **sum** has three infinitives. Here are their forms:

TENSE	INFINITIVE	MEANING
PRESENT	esse	*to be*
PERFECT	fuisse	*to have been*
FUTURE	fūtūrum esse	*to be going to be*

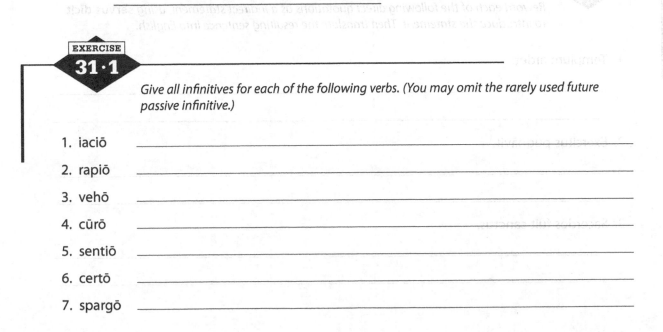

EXERCISE
31·1

Give all infinitives for each of the following verbs. (You may omit the rarely used future passive infinitive.)

1. iaciō _____

2. rapiō _____

3. vehō _____

4. cūrō _____

5. sentiō _____

6. certō _____

7. spargō _____

8. exerceō _____

9. ostendō _____

10. ēligō _____

Indirect statement

The most common use of infinitives, besides the complementary infinitive and the infinitive as subject or object, is in indirect statement. Indirect statement is the common process of repeating someone else's words, but in such a way that you do not quote them directly. Indirect statement usually follows a verb that conveys the notion of speaking, thinking, sensing, or other mental activity.

DIRECT STATEMENT	INDIRECT STATEMENT
Augustus: *I heard it.*	*The slave says that Augustus heard it.*
Augustus: Id audīvī.	Servus dīcit Augustum id audīvisse.

In English, we usually add the word *that* to signal indirect statement, but otherwise don't make many other changes. In Latin, indirect statement is marked by a specific change of case and verb form.

	SUBJECT	VERB
DIRECT STATEMENT	NOMINATIVE CASE Ego [Augustus]	CONJUGATED FORM audīvī
INDIRECT STATEMENT	ACCUSATIVE CASE Augustum	CORRESPONDING INFINITIVE audīvisse

EXERCISE 31·2

Reword each of the following direct quotations as a indirect statement, using **servus dīcit** *to introduce the statement. Then translate the resulting sentence into English.*

1. Templum ardet.

   _____

   _____

2. Exercitus pugnāvit.

   _____

   _____

3. Sacerdōs fuit sanctus.

   _____

   _____

4. Animālia cornua possunt habēre.

_____

_____

5. Ōrātiō placēbit.

_____

_____

6. Tū mē amās.

_____

_____

7. Cohors victa est.

_____

_____

8. Verba nostra sunt inānia.

_____

_____

9. Pax petīta erat.

_____

_____

10. Custōdēs dormiunt nec vigilant.

_____

_____

Numbers

Like English, Latin has two sets of numbers: *cardinal numbers*, used for counting, and *ordinal numbers*, used for ranking.

Cardinal numbers

Most of the cardinal numbers are indeclinable. Each cardinal number between 4 and 100 has only one form, which doesn't change regardless of case. Multiples of 100 follow the pattern of **-us -a -um** adjectives in the plural (**-ī -ae -a**).

The forms for the cardinal numbers 1, 2, and 3 change for case and gender. Here are their declensions:

The number 1

CASE	MASCULINE	FEMININE	NEUTER
NOMINATIVE	ūnus	ūna	ūnum
GENITIVE	ūnīus	ūnīus	ūnīus
DATIVE	ūnī	ūnī	ūnī
ACCUSATIVE	ūnum	ūnam	ūnum
ABLATIVE	ūnō	ūnā	ūnō
VOCATIVE	ūne	ūna	ūnum

The number 2

CASE	MASCULINE	FEMININE	NEUTER
NOMINATIVE	duo	duae	duo
GENITIVE	duōrum	duārum	duōrum
DATIVE	duōbus	duābus	duōbus
ACCUSATIVE	duōs	duās	duo
ABLATIVE	duōbus	duābus	duōbus
VOCATIVE	duo	duae	duo

The number 3

CASE	MASCULINE/ FEMININE	NEUTER
NOMINATIVE	trēs	tria
GENITIVE	trium	trium
DATIVE	tribus	tribus
ACCUSATIVE	trēs	tria
ABLATIVE	tribus	tribus
VOCATIVE	trēs	tria

Following is a list of important cardinal numbers between 1 and 1,000. The numbers 21 through 29 can be used as a model for 31 through 39, 41 through 49, and so on.

1	ūnus ūna ūnum		30	trīgintā
2	duo duae duo		40	quadrāgintā
3	trēs tria		50	quinquāgintā
4	quattuor		60	sexāgintā
5	quinque		70	septuāgintā
6	sex		80	octōgintā
7	septem		90	nōnāgintā
8	octō		100	centum
9	novem		200	ducentī -ae -a
10	decem		300	trecentī -ae -a
11	undecim		400	quadringentī -ae -a
12	duodecim		500	quingentī -ae -a
13	tredecim		600	sescentī -ae -a
14	quattuordecim		700	septingentī -ae -a
15	quindecim		800	octingentī -ae -a
16	sēdecim		900	nongentī -ae -a
17	septendecim		1,000	mille
18	duodēvīgintī			
19	undēvīgintī			
20	vīgintī			
21	vīgintī ūnus			
22	vīgintī duo			
23	vīgintī trēs			
24	vīgintī quattuor			
25	vīgintī quinque			
26	vīgintī sex			
27	vīgintī septem			
28	vīgintī octō			
29	vīgintī novem			

Ordinal numbers

Ordinal numbers rank items or put them in numerical order. They all are adjectives ending in **-us -a -um**. Here is a list of important ordinal numbers from 1st to 100th. The number 13th shows the pattern for numbers between multiples of ten.

1st	prīmus -a -um
2nd	secundus -a -um
3rd	tertius -a -um
4th	quartus -a -um
5th	quintus -a -um
6th	sextus -a -um
7th	septimus -a -um
8th	octāvus -a -um
9th	nōnus -a -um
10th	decimus -a -um
11th	undecimus -a -um
12th	duodecimus -a -um
13th	tertius decimus tertia decima tertium decimum
20th	vīcensimus -a -um
30th	trīcensimus -a -um
40th	quadrāgensimus -a -um
50th	quinquāgensimus -a -um
60th	sexāgensimus -a -um
70th	septuāgensimus -a -um
80th	octōgensimus -a -um
90th	nōnāgensimus -a -um
100th	centensimus -a -um

EXERCISE
32·1

Translate each of the following numbers into Latin.

1. thirty-third _____

2. 27 _____

3. seventh _____

4. first _____

5. 10 _____

6. 50 _____

7. 500 _____

8. fifth _____

9. forty-second _____

10. 648 _____

Give the arabic numeral for each of the following numbers, then transform a cardinal number to its Latin ordinal equivalent, or vice versa.

1. trīcensimus _____

2. duodēvīgintī _____

3. centum _____

4. quīnquāgintā octō _____

5. quattuor _____

6. nōnāgensimus tertius _____

7. septimus _____

8. sēdecim _____

9. octāvus _____

10. quinquāgensimus sextus _____

Translate each of the following phrases into Latin.

1. two eyes (*nom.*) _____

2. first old man (*acc.*) _____

3. fifteen days (*abl.*) _____

4. twenty rocks (*dat.*) _____

5. one empire (*acc.*) _____

6. fourth hour (*nom.*) _____

7. seventh son (*dat.*) _____

8. twenty-fifth war (*acc.*) _____

9. three goddesses (*gen.*) _____

10. one thousand soldiers (*nom.*) _____

Expressions of time

Rather than using prepositional phrases like *on the fifth day*, *within a few hours*, *in the summer*, or *for seven years*, Latin uses case endings alone to indicate these expressions of time.

Time when

To express the time when something occurred, Latin uses the ablative case.

Vēre et hieme labōrāmus.	*We work in the spring and the winter.*
Prīmā lūce exeunt.	*They are leaving at first light.*

Time within which

To express the period of time within which something occurred, Latin uses the ablative case.

Novem annīs moenia cadent.	*The walls will fall within nine years.*
Brevī tempore hostēs pervēnērunt.	*The enemies arrived within a short time.*

Duration of time

To express the amount of time that something lasted, Latin uses the accusative case.

Decem annōs in urbe pugnābant.	*They were fighting in the city for ten years.*
In Italiā sex diēs manēbis.	*You will remain in Italy for six days.*

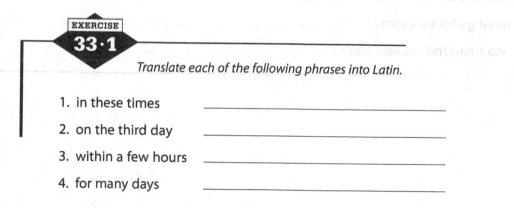

EXERCISE

33·1

Translate each of the following phrases into Latin.

1. in these times _____

2. on the third day _____

3. within a few hours _____

4. for many days _____

5. at first light   _____

6. in my age   _____

7. for so many hours   _____

8. on the following night   _____

9. within this winter   _____

10. for a short time   _____

EXERCISE 33·2

Translate each of the following sentences into English.

1. Hīs temporibus rex noster fuit.

2. Proximō diē librōs ad Galliam mīsit.

3. Quadrāgintā noctēs vigilāvī tē exspectans.

4. Eōdem tempore quisque suam cīvitātem dēserēbat.

5. Diē quartō equus niger nātus est.

6. Nostrā aetāte Rōma nōn vincētur.

7. Paucīs hōrīs nuntium currentem vīdērunt.

8. Multōs annōs urbs Trōia ab hostibus cincta est.

9. Septem hōrās sub sōle pugnābat.

10. Diem tōtum ōrātiōnem audīre cōnātus sum.

Questions

Latin generally marks questions with a question word at the beginning of a sentence or clause. The most common questions ask *who?*, *what?*, or *which one?* and use the interrogative pronoun or interrogative adjective.

The interrogative pronoun

The interrogative pronoun asks *who?* (masculine or feminine) or *what?* (neuter). Its forms are very similar to the forms of the relative pronoun.

NUMBER	CASE	MASCULINE	FEMININE	NEUTER
SINGULAR	NOMINATIVE	quis	quis	quid
	GENITIVE	cuius	cuius	cuius
	DATIVE	cui	cui	cui
	ACCUSATIVE	quem	quem	quid
	ABLATIVE	quō	quō	quō
PLURAL	NOMINATIVE	quī	quae	quae
	GENITIVE	quōrum	quārum	quōrum
	DATIVE	quibus	quibus	quibus
	ACCUSATIVE	quōs	quās	quae
	ABLATIVE	quibus	quibus	quibus

Notice that the feminine forms are the same as the masculine ones in the singular, but not in the plural.

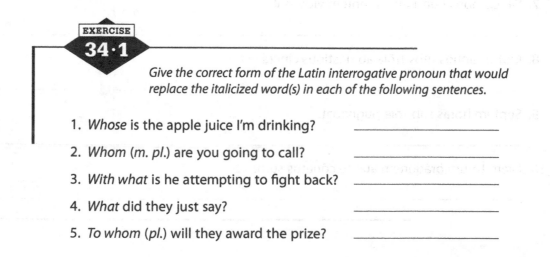

EXERCISE 34·1

Give the correct form of the Latin interrogative pronoun that would replace the italicized word(s) in each of the following sentences.

1. *Whose* is the apple juice I'm drinking? _____

2. *Whom (m. pl.)* are you going to call? _____

3. *With what* is he attempting to fight back? _____

4. *What* did they just say? _____

5. *To whom (pl.)* will they award the prize? _____

6. *Who* (*f. pl.*) told you that lie? _____

7. *Whose* property are we standing on? _____

8. *What* causes this sort of malady? _____

9. *With whom* (*pl.*) did they attend the party? _____

10. *Who* ate my cookies? _____

The interrogative adjective

The interrogative adjective modifies a noun, using the same case, number, and gender as the noun. Its forms are identical to those of the relative pronoun.

NUMBER	CASE	MASCULINE	FEMININE	NEUTER
SINGULAR	NOMINATIVE	quī	quae	quod
	GENITIVE	cuius	cuius	cuius
	DATIVE	cui	cui	cui
	ACCUSATIVE	quem	quam	quod
	ABLATIVE	quō	quā	quō
PLURAL	NOMINATIVE	quī	quae	quae
	GENITIVE	quōrum	quārum	quōrum
	DATIVE	quibus	quibus	quibus
	ACCUSATIVE	quōs	quās	quae
	ABLATIVE	quibus	quibus	quibus

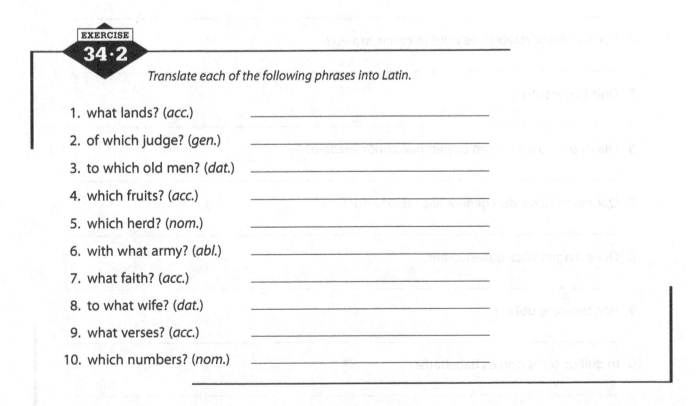

EXERCISE 34·2

Translate each of the following phrases into Latin.

1. what lands? (*acc.*) _____

2. of which judge? (*gen.*) _____

3. to which old men? (*dat.*) _____

4. which fruits? (*acc.*) _____

5. which herd? (*nom.*) _____

6. with what army? (*abl.*) _____

7. what faith? (*acc.*) _____

8. to what wife? (*dat.*) _____

9. what verses? (*acc.*) _____

10. which numbers? (*nom.*) _____

Other question words

Latin can, of course, ask questions other than *who?* or *what?* Here is a list of words commonly used to introduce questions:

ubi	*where? when?*	quandō	*when?*
unde	*from where?*	quōmodo	*how?*
cūr	*why?*	quīn	*why not . . . ?*
quālis -e	*what kind?*	quārē	*in what way? how?*
quantus -a -um	*how great?*	quō	*to where?*

The suffix **-ne** may be attached to the beginning word of a question to indicate that the sentence is a question. **-Ne** has no meaning itself.

Estne hīc fēmina?	*Is the woman here?*
Vīvuntne illī hominēs?	*Are those men living?*

EXERCISE

34·3

Translate each of the following sentences into English.

1. Unde ille praemium dedit?

_____

2. Cuius auxilium ad exercitum mīsistī?

_____

3. Cui diem festum reddēbant?

_____

4. Cūr nōn immortālibus rēs publica commissa est?

_____

5. Quis hoc instituit?

_____

6. Quem tamquam malum turpemque cōnor ēvādere?

_____

7. Quōmodo igitur duo genera haec dīvīdentur?

_____

8. Quae magnā vōce quaesīverant?

_____

9. Hōc tempore ubi es?

_____

10. In quibus terrīs domōs habēbātis?

_____

Mood is the last of the characteristics of Latin verbs to be studied. Mood indicates the relationship of a verb (and therefore the sentence) to reality or factuality. All the verbs you have studied so far have been in the indicative mood, which is used to make plain, factual statements. The other moods are imperative and subjunctive. (Some people consider the infinitive a mood as well.) Latin marks moods by a change in form.

The imperative mood

The imperative mood is used to give commands. Because commands attempt to make something happen and don't just state plain facts, they cannot use the indicative. Commands are generally in the second person and may be singular or plural. Here is the formula for the imperative mood in Latin:

Present system root = Imperative singular

Present system root + **-te** = Imperative plural

	CONJUGATION				
	FIRST	SECOND	THIRD	THIRD **-iō**	FOURTH
SECOND PERSON SINGULAR	amā	tenē	pōne	cape	audī
SECOND PERSON PLURAL	amāte	tenēte	pōnite	capite	audīte

Note that the weak root vowel of the third and third **-iō** conjugations changes to **-i-** in the imperative plural.

Negative commands

To give a negative command (*don't!*), Latin uses a different formula.

nōlī + Present active infinitive = Negative imperative singular

nōlīte + Present active infinitive = Negative imperative plural

Here are examples of command sentences:

Tolle hoc pondus!   *Lift this weight!*
Nōlī eam contemnere!   *Don't condemn her!*

Give the imperative form of each of the following verbs.

1. respondeō (*sg.*) _____
2. videō (*pl.*) _____
3. errō (*sg.*) _____
4. taceō (*pl.*) _____
5. vigilō (*sg.*) _____
6. conveniō (*sg.*) _____
7. addō (*sg.*) _____
8. surgō (*sg.*) _____
9. discēdō (*sg.*) _____
10. agō (*pl.*) _____

Translate each of the following imperatives into Latin.

1. rejoice! (*pl.*) _____
2. remain! (*sg.*) _____
3. weep! (*pl.*) _____
4. come! (*sg.*) _____
5. read! (*sg.*) _____
6. don't pour! (*sg.*) _____
7. sing! (*sg.*) _____
8. don't laugh! (*pl.*) _____
9. kill! (*sg.*) _____
10. stand! (*pl.*) _____

Translate each of the following imperatives into English.

1. suscipite _____

2. prōmitte _____

3. nōlī convertere _____

4. venī _____

5. servāte _____

6. nōlīte iacēre _____

7. scīte _____

8. intrā _____

9. certāte _____

10. aperī _____

The subjunctive mood

The subjunctive mood is used to talk about the possible, the ideal, and the counterfactual. The exact meaning of the subjunctive in a sentence is determined by several factors in the context. The following chapters cover some of the most important and common uses of the subjunctive mood.

Latin marks verbs and sentences that express these kinds of ideas by changing the form of the verb. To negate a subjunctive verb, Latin usually (but not always) uses **nē** instead of **nōn**. Almost every indicative verb form has a corresponding subjunctive form, with the exception that there are no future subjunctives.

The present subjunctive active tense

To form the present subjunctive, the vowel sounds at the end of the verb root are changed according to the following pattern.

| | CONJUGATION | | | | |
	FIRST	SECOND	THIRD	THIRD **-iŏ**	FOURTH
INDICATIVE VOWEL SOUND	ā	ē	e/i	e/i	ī
PRESENT SUBJUNCTIVE VOWEL SOUND	ē	eā	ā	iā	iā

Following are example charts of the present subjunctive active for each conjugation. Note that the subjunctive cannot be translated out of context.

First conjugation

amō, amāre, amāvī, amātum *love*

	SINGULAR	PLURAL
FIRST PERSON	amem	amēmus
SECOND PERSON	amēs	amētis
THIRD PERSON	amet	ament

Second conjugation

teneō, tenēre, tenuī, tentum *hold*

	SINGULAR	PLURAL
FIRST PERSON	teneam	teneāmus
SECOND PERSON	teneās	teneātis
THIRD PERSON	teneat	teneant

Third conjugation

pōnō, pōnere, posuī, positum *put*

	SINGULAR	PLURAL
FIRST PERSON	pōnam	pōnāmus
SECOND PERSON	pōnās	pōnātis
THIRD PERSON	pōnat	pōnant

Third -iō conjugation

capiō, capere, cēpī, captum *take*

	SINGULAR	PLURAL
FIRST PERSON	capiam	capiāmus
SECOND PERSON	capiās	capiātis
THIRD PERSON	capiat	capiant

Fourth conjugation

audiō, audīre, audīvī, audītum *hear*

	SINGULAR	PLURAL
FIRST PERSON	audiam	audiāmus
SECOND PERSON	audiās	audiātis
THIRD PERSON	audiat	audiant

EXERCISE 36·1

Identify the person, number, tense, and mood of each of the following verbs.

1. ardeant _____

2. accidant _____

3. cernās _____

4. sonent _____

5. serviātis _____

6. cavet _____

7. conficiēs _____

8. cessent _____

9. linquit _____

10. praestem _____

The present subjunctive passive tense

The present subjunctive passive follows the same pattern as the corresponding indicative tense. The present subjunctive vowel sounds are substituted for the indicative ones. Here are example charts of the present subjunctive passive for each conjugation:

First conjugation

amō, amāre, amāvī, amātum *love*

	SINGULAR	PLURAL
FIRST PERSON	amer	amēmur
SECOND PERSON	amēris	amēminī
THIRD PERSON	amētur	amentur

Second conjugation

teneō, tenēre, tenuī, tentum *hold*

	SINGULAR	PLURAL
FIRST PERSON	tenear	teneāmur
SECOND PERSON	teneāris	teneāminī
THIRD PERSON	teneātur	teneantur

Third conjugation

pōnō, pōnere, posuī, positum *put*

	SINGULAR	PLURAL
FIRST PERSON	pōnar	pōnāmur
SECOND PERSON	pōnāris	pōnāminī
THIRD PERSON	pōnātur	pōnantur

Third -iō conjugation

capiō, capere, cēpī, captum *take*

	SINGULAR	PLURAL
FIRST PERSON	capiar	capiāmur
SECOND PERSON	capiāris	capiāminī
THIRD PERSON	capiātur	capiantur

Fourth conjugation

audiō, audīre, audīvī, audītum *hear*

	SINGULAR	PLURAL
FIRST PERSON	audiar	audiāmur
SECOND PERSON	audiāris	audiāminī
THIRD PERSON	audiātur	audiantur

Identify the person, number, tense, and mood of each of the following passive verbs.

1. nesciātur   _____
2. lūdentur   _____
3. ascendāmur   _____
4. bibātur   _____
5. vertiminī   _____
6. rapiantur   _____
7. aspiciēris   _____
8. iubear   _____
9. rumpentur   _____
10. revocātur   _____

The imperfect subjunctive active tense

The imperfect subjunctive is formed by adding the active personal endings to the present active infinitive. Here are example charts of the imperfect subjunctive active for each conjugation:

First conjugation

amō, amāre, amāvī, amātum *love*

	SINGULAR	PLURAL
FIRST PERSON	**amāre**m	**amāre**mus
SECOND PERSON	**amāre**s	**amāre**tis
THIRD PERSON	**amāre**t	**amāre**nt

Second conjugation

teneō, tenēre, tenuī, tentum *hold*

	SINGULAR	PLURAL
FIRST PERSON	**tenēre**m	**tenēre**mus
SECOND PERSON	**tenēre**s	**tenēre**tis
THIRD PERSON	**tenēre**t	**tenēre**nt

Third conjugation

pōnō, pōnere, posuī, positum *put*

	SINGULAR	PLURAL
FIRST PERSON	**pōnere**m	**pōnere**mus
SECOND PERSON	**pōnere**s	**pōnere**tis
THIRD PERSON	**pōnere**t	**pōnere**nt

Third -iō conjugation

capiō, capere, cēpī, captum *take*

	SINGULAR	PLURAL
FIRST PERSON	**capere**m	**capere**̄mus
SECOND PERSON	**capere**̄s	**capere**̄tis
THIRD PERSON	**capere**t	**capere**nt

Fourth conjugation

audiō, audīre, audīvī, audītum *hear*

	SINGULAR	PLURAL
FIRST PERSON	**audīre**m	**audīre**̄mus
SECOND PERSON	**audīre**̄s	**audīre**̄tis
THIRD PERSON	**audīre**t	**audīre**nt

**EXERCISE
36·3**

Identify the person, number, tense, and mood of each of the following verbs.

1. manēbam   _____

2. cēdēs   _____

3. cresceret   _____

4. parcerem   _____

5. sedēret   _____

6. vīverēs   _____

7. prōdat   _____

8. vacārent   _____

9. quiescerēmus   _____

10. venīrent   _____

The imperfect subjunctive passive tense

The imperfect subjunctive passive is formed by adding passive personal endings to the present active infinitive. Here are example charts of the imperfect subjunctive passive for each conjugation:

First conjugation

amō, amāre, amāvī, amātum *love*

	SINGULAR	PLURAL
FIRST PERSON	**amāre**r	**amāre**̄mur
SECOND PERSON	**amāre**̄ris	**amāre**̄minī
THIRD PERSON	**amāre**̄tur	**amāre**ntur

Second conjugation

teneō, tenēre, tenuī, tentum *hold*

	SINGULAR	PLURAL
FIRST PERSON	**tenērer**	**tenērēmur**
SECOND PERSON	**tenērēris**	**tenērēminī**
THIRD PERSON	**tenērētur**	**tenērentur**

Third conjugation

pōnō, pōnere, posuī, positum *put*

	SINGULAR	PLURAL
FIRST PERSON	**pōnerer**	**pōnerēmur**
SECOND PERSON	**pōnerēris**	**pōnerēminī**
THIRD PERSON	**pōnerētur**	**pōnerentur**

Third -iō conjugation

capiō, capere, cēpī, captum *take*

	SINGULAR	PLURAL
FIRST PERSON	**caperer**	**caperēmur**
SECOND PERSON	**caperēris**	**caperēminī**
THIRD PERSON	**caperētur**	**caperentur**

Fourth conjugation

audiō, audīre, audīvī, audītum *hear*

	SINGULAR	PLURAL
FIRST PERSON	**audīrer**	**audīrēmur**
SECOND PERSON	**audīrēris**	**audīrēminī**
THIRD PERSON	**audīrētur**	**audīrentur**

EXERCISE

36·4

Identify the person, number, tense, and mood of each of the following passive verbs.

1. sustinērēminī _____

2. funderentur _____

3. sūmimur _____

4. negārētur _____

5. contingantur _____

6. quaererēris _____

7. cūrārer _____

8. exciperētur _____

9. implērēris _____

10. audīrentur _____

The perfect subjunctive active tense

The perfect subjunctive active uses the perfect active root (from the third principal part). To that root is added the tense marker **-eri-** and the active personal endings. With the exception of the first person singular form (and the long **-ī-** in the endings of the second person singular and first and second persons plural), the perfect subjunctive active looks exactly like the future perfect indicative. Here are example charts of the perfect subjunctive active for each conjugation:

First conjugation

amō, amāre, amāvī, amātum *love*

	SINGULAR	PLURAL
FIRST PERSON	amā**verim**	amā**verīmus**
SECOND PERSON	amā**verīs**	amā**verītis**
THIRD PERSON	amā**verit**	amā**verint**

Second conjugation

teneō, tenēre, tenuī, tentum *hold*

	SINGULAR	PLURAL
FIRST PERSON	tenu**erim**	tenu**erīmus**
SECOND PERSON	tenu**erīs**	tenu**erītis**
THIRD PERSON	tenu**erit**	tenu**erint**

Third conjugation

pōnō, pōnere, posuī, positum *put*

	SINGULAR	PLURAL
FIRST PERSON	posu**erim**	posu**erīmus**
SECOND PERSON	posu**erīs**	posu**erītis**
THIRD PERSON	posu**erit**	posu**erint**

Third -iō conjugation

capiō, capere, cēpī, captum *take*

	SINGULAR	PLURAL
FIRST PERSON	cēp**erim**	cēp**erīmus**
SECOND PERSON	cēp**erīs**	cēp**erītis**
THIRD PERSON	cēp**erit**	cēp**erint**

Fourth conjugation

audiō, audīre, audīvī, audītum *hear*

	SINGULAR	PLURAL
FIRST PERSON	audī**verim**	audī**verīmus**
SECOND PERSON	audī**verīs**	audī**verītis**
THIRD PERSON	audī**verit**	audī**verint**

Identify the person, number, tense, and mood of each of the following verbs.

1. dedistī _____

2. steterim _____

3. placuit _____

4. cantāveram _____

5. condidī _____

6. repperērunt _____

7. fūgerīs _____

8. doluerītis _____

9. dēfēcerit _____

10. appāruerint _____

The pluperfect subjunctive active tense

The pluperfect subjunctive active is formed by adding the active personal endings to the perfect active infinitive. Here are example charts of the pluperfect subjunctive active for each conjugation:

First conjugation

amō, amāre, amāvī, amātum *love*

	SINGULAR	PLURAL
FIRST PERSON	amāvissem	amāvissēmus
SECOND PERSON	amāvissēs	amāvissētis
THIRD PERSON	amāvisset	amāvissent

Second conjugation

teneō, tenēre, tenuī, tentum *hold*

	SINGULAR	PLURAL
FIRST PERSON	tenuissem	tenuissēmus
SECOND PERSON	tenuissēs	tenuissētis
THIRD PERSON	tenuisset	tenuissent

Third conjugation

pōnō, pōnere, posuī, positum *put*

	SINGULAR	PLURAL
FIRST PERSON	posuissem	posuissēmus
SECOND PERSON	posuissēs	posuissētis
THIRD PERSON	posuisset	posuissent

Third -iō conjugation

capiō, capere, cēpī, captum *take*

	SINGULAR	PLURAL
FIRST PERSON	cēpissem	cēpissēmus
SECOND PERSON	cēpissēs	cēpissētis
THIRD PERSON	cēpisset	cēpissent

Fourth conjugation

audiō, audīre, audīvī, audītum *hear*

	SINGULAR	PLURAL
FIRST PERSON	audīvissem	audīvissēmus
SECOND PERSON	audīvissēs	audīvissētis
THIRD PERSON	audīvisset	audīvissent

EXERCISE

36·6

Identify the person, number, tense, and mood of each of the following verbs.

1. strāverim _____

2. fefellissem _____

3. ēvāserās _____

4. compārāvissent _____

5. coluērunt _____

6. valuissent _____

7. interfēcisset _____

8. respexit _____

9. memorāvissēs _____

10. patuissem _____

The perfect subjunctive passive tense

The perfect subjunctive passive uses the perfect passive system root from the fourth principal part. Like the perfect passive indicative, it is composed of two words. The first word is an -us -a -um adjective modifying the subject. The second word is a present subjunctive form of sum. Here are example charts of the perfect subjunctive passive for each conjugation:

First conjugation

amō, amāre, amāvī, amātum *love*
GENDER OF SUBJECT   Masculine

	SINGULAR	PLURAL
FIRST PERSON	amātus **sim**	amātī **sīmus**
SECOND PERSON	amātus **sīs**	amātī **sītis**
THIRD PERSON	amātus **sit**	amātī **sint**

Second conjugation

teneō, tenēre, tenuī, tentum *hold*
GENDER OF SUBJECT   Masculine

	SINGULAR	PLURAL
FIRST PERSON	tentus **sim**	tentī **sīmus**
SECOND PERSON	tentus **sīs**	tentī **sītis**
THIRD PERSON	tentus **sit**	tentī **sint**

Third conjugation

pōnō, pōnere, posuī, positum *put*
GENDER OF SUBJECT   Feminine

	SINGULAR	PLURAL
FIRST PERSON	posita **sim**	positae **sīmus**
SECOND PERSON	posita **sīs**	positae **sītis**
THIRD PERSON	posita **sit**	positae **sint**

Third -iō conjugation

capiō, capere, cēpī, captum *take*
GENDER OF SUBJECT   Neuter

	SINGULAR	PLURAL
FIRST PERSON	captum **sim**	capta **sīmus**
SECOND PERSON	captum **sīs**	capta **sītis**
THIRD PERSON	captum **sit**	capta **sint**

Fourth conjugation

audiō, audīre, audīvī, audītum *hear*
GENDER OF SUBJECT   Masculine

	SINGULAR	PLURAL
FIRST PERSON	audītus **sim**	audītī **sīmus**
SECOND PERSON	audītus **sīs**	audītī **sītis**
THIRD PERSON	audītus **sit**	audītī **sint**

Identify the person, number, tense, and mood of each of the following verbs.

1. probātus est _____

2. iactus sim _____

3. petīta erat _____

4. merīta erunt _____

5. pensa sit _____

6. mūtātae sītis _____

7. redditum est _____

8. institūtum sit _____

9. monitī sīmus _____

10. coactī sint _____

The pluperfect subjunctive passive tense

The pluperfect subjunctive passive is built from the perfect passive system root plus the imperfect subjunctive tense of **sum**. Here are example charts of the pluperfect subjunctive passive for each conjugation:

First conjugation

amō, amāre, amāvī, amātum *love*
GENDER OF SUBJECT   Masculine

	SINGULAR	PLURAL
FIRST PERSON	amātus **essem**	amātī **essēmus**
SECOND PERSON	amātus **essēs**	amātī **essētis**
THIRD PERSON	amātus **esset**	amātī **essent**

Second conjugation

teneō, tenēre, tenuī, tentum *hold*
GENDER OF SUBJECT   Masculine

	SINGULAR	PLURAL
FIRST PERSON	tentus **essem**	tentī **essēmus**
SECOND PERSON	tentus **essēs**	tentī **essētis**
THIRD PERSON	tentus **esset**	tentī **essent**

Third conjugation

pōnō, pōnere, posuī, positum *put*
GENDER OF SUBJECT Feminine

	SINGULAR	PLURAL
FIRST PERSON	posita **essem**	positae **essēmus**
SECOND PERSON	posita **essēs**	positae **essētis**
THIRD PERSON	posita **esset**	positae **essent**

Third -iō conjugation

capiō, capere, cēpī, captum *take*
GENDER OF SUBJECT Neuter

	SINGULAR	PLURAL
FIRST PERSON	captum **essem**	capta **essēmus**
SECOND PERSON	captum **essēs**	capta **essētis**
THIRD PERSON	captum **esset**	capta **essent**

Fourth conjugation

audiō, audīre, audīvī, audītum *hear*
GENDER OF SUBJECT Masculine

	SINGULAR	PLURAL
FIRST PERSON	audītus **essem**	audītī **essēmus**
SECOND PERSON	audītus **essēs**	audītī **essētis**
THIRD PERSON	audītus **esset**	audītī **essent**

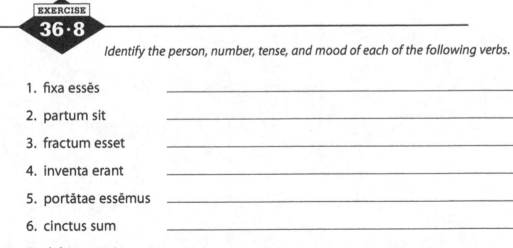

EXERCISE 36·8

Identify the person, number, tense, and mood of each of the following verbs.

1. fixa essēs _____

2. partum sit _____

3. fractum esset _____

4. inventa erant _____

5. portātae essēmus _____

6. cinctus sum _____

7. dēbitī essētis _____

8. sepultus essem _____

9. vectus erit _____

10. nōminātī essent _____

Identify the person, number, tense, voice, and mood of each of the following verbs.

1. videant _____

2. līberāta sit _____

3. cupīverit _____

4. scrīpsissēmus _____

5. indūta essent _____

6. solvēbātur _____

7. fluerent _____

8. ductī sunt _____

9. āmissus sīs _____

10. claudent _____

Independent subjunctives  **·37·**

If the idea that a sentence expresses is possible, ideal, or counterfactual, Latin sometimes uses a subjunctive verb as the main verb of the sentence. In these cases, the verb is one of the following types:

1. *Hortatory/jussive subjunctive*, indicating that the verb is a command
2. *Optative subjunctive*, indicating that the verb expresses a wish
3. *Deliberative subjunctive*, indicating that the verb expresses a thought about a possible action
4. *Potential subjunctive*, indicating that the verb action *could* or *might* be true

These are the most common uses of the subjunctive as the verb in an independent clause.

The hortatory/jussive subjunctive

The hortatory/jussive subjunctive is the most common of this group. Unlike the second-person commands of the imperative mood, these subjunctives express commands in the first and third persons. Commands in the first person are called *hortatory subjunctives* (you "exhort" yourself to do something), and commands in the third person are called *jussive subjunctives*. The English translation is usually *Let me/us / him/her/it/them* _____.

Vīvāmus atque amēmus.	*Let us live and love.*
Discēdant omnēs.	*Let them all leave.*

Identify the person, number, tense, voice, and mood of each of the following verbs.

1. constant _____

2. dīcātur _____

3. recipiēris _____

4. impleāmur _____

5. fluunt _____

6. vīvātis _____

7. perveniant _____

8. frangās _____

9. mittat _____

10. celebrātur _____

Translate each of the following verb phrases into Latin.

1. let them approve _____

2. let him be taught _____

3. let it burn _____

4. let me attempt _____

5. let us ask for _____

6. let her be _____

7. let him be careful _____

8. let us follow _____

9. let me drink _____

10. let them run _____

Translate each of the following sentences into English.

1. Sē servet ille vir sine amīcīs.

_____

2. Sed tōtam rem efficiāmus, quia incēpimus.

_____

3. Mīlitēs per hiemem quoque exerceant.

_____

4. Terra sit tibi levis.

_____

5. Intrā rumpam in templum.

_____

6. Cernat sē beātum fūtūrum esse.

_____

7. Fidem meam ad omnia parātam esse putent.

_____

8. Surguntne hōc tempore sīdera?

_____

9. Pondus ab aquā nōn sustinētur.

_____

10. Deam puerī puellaeque canāmus.

_____

·38· Dependent subjunctives • Purpose clauses

Latin uses the subjunctive to mark certain dependent clauses that carry nonfactual meaning. There is a large variety to these clauses. Here are the major types of dependent subjunctive clauses:

1. *Purpose clause*, which indicates the purpose of the action in the independent clause
2. *Result clause*, which indicates a natural and necessary consequence of the action in the independent clause
3. **Cum**-*clause*, which adds information about the cause, time, or circumstances of the action in the independent clause
4. *Indirect question*, which contains a question that is not asked directly
5. *Indirect command*, which contains a command that is not given directly
6. *Fear clause*, which expresses the object of a fear
7. *Conditional clause*, which sets the condition under which the independent clause is true or viable
8. *Proviso clause*, which limits the truth of the independent clause to a specific set of conditions

Purpose clauses

Purpose clauses are one of the most common types of dependent subjunctive clauses. This clause expresses the reason for or the purpose of the action in the independent clause. A purpose clause is introduced by the subordinating conjunction *ut* (or *nē*, if the clause expresses a negative idea).

Imperātor adest ut fābulam audiat.	*The emperor is present in order to hear the story.* (Hearing the story is the purpose of the emperor's presence.)
Arbōrem ascendit nē inveniātur.	*He is climbing the tree so that he won't be found.* (His not being found is the purpose of climbing the tree.)

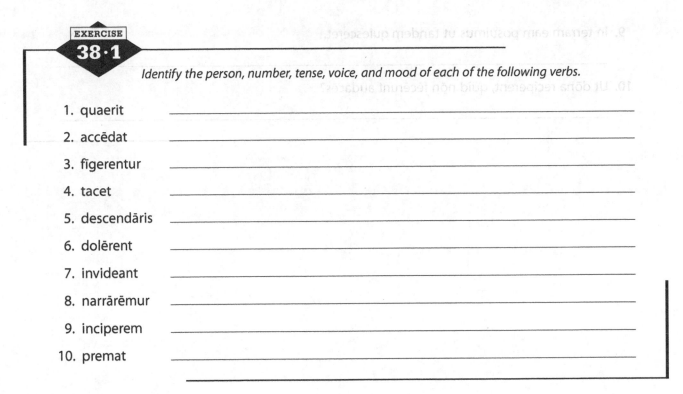

EXERCISE 38·1

Identify the person, number, tense, voice, and mood of each of the following verbs.

1. quaerit _____

2. accēdat _____

3. fīgerentur _____

4. tacet _____

5. descendāris _____

6. dolērent _____

7. invideant _____

8. narrārēmur _____

9. inciperem _____

10. premat _____

EXERCISE 38·2

Translate each of the following sentences into English.

1. Silvās petō ut silentiō dormiam.

   _____

2. Nocte pecūniam rapuit nē mala eius intellegerentur.

   _____

3. Vēra verba retinuistī ut nōs fallerēs.

   _____

4. Hostēs occīdimus ut lībera maneat urbs.

   _____

5. Ōs claudit nē illīs respondeat.

   _____

6. Pōne flōrēs in mediā mensā ut ab omnibus vidērī possint.

   _____

7. Tibi attulī auxilium ut nōs amīcī essēmus.

   _____

8. Dominus in agrōs properat ut servōs fugientēs capiat.

   _____

9. In terram eam posuimus ut tandem quiesceret.

_____

10. Ut dōna reciperent, quid nōn fēcērunt audācēs?

_____

Cum-clauses

This common dependent clause is introduced by the subordinating conjunction **cum**. (Be careful not to confuse this with the preposition **cum**.) A **cum**-clause adds information about the circumstances of the action in the independent clause—ideas that English would express with words like the following:

1. *Because/since*
2. *When/while/as*
3. *Although*

Here are example sentences:

> Cum rēs tam malae sint, nemō consilium capit.
> *Because things are so bad, no one is coming up with a plan.*
> Cum exercitus victus sit, urbs cadet.
> *When the army is defeated, the city will fall.*

If the verb in a **cum**-clause is indicative, the clause expresses precise time (*when*). But if the verb is subjunctive, context will indicate which of the above ideas the clause is expressing. It can sometimes be difficult to choose, since two ideas may seem equally valid, or even mixed.

EXERCISE
39·1

Identify the person, number, tense, voice, and mood of each of the following verbs.

1. complectēbāmur _____

2. concēdant _____

3. possētis _____

4. dēsīderāverant _____

5. institūtī sīmus _____

6. indicat _____

7. reperta esset _____

8. dīligāminī _____

9. patēbant _____

10. excēpistis _____

Translate each of the following sentences into English.

1. Cum bellum mīlitēs gererent, dux illīs imperābat.

   _____

2. Cum tōtā nocte vigilārem, inventa est tamen ops nostra et ablāta est.

   _____

3. Cum terram nōn videat, ad lītora tamen pervenīre spērant.

   _____

4. Cum rusticus haec dixisset, omnēs rīsērunt.

   _____

5. Cum illa deum maris timeat, semper nāvēs cavet.

   _____

6. Cum locūtus esset, vox eius dēfēcit.

   _____

7. Cum hoc fēcisset, ad tē fūgit plūra exspectans.

   _____

8. Cum multī fīliī in proeliīs mortuī sint, ūnus tamen remanet.

   _____

9. Cum corpus in rogō ardet, māter sorōrēsque flent.

   _____

10. Cum audientēs cunctī tacērent, fābulam mīram narrābās.

   _____

Conditional sentences

Conditional sentences (of the form *if . . . then*) are used to describe real, possible, or counterfactual situations in the past, present, or future. As you might expect, Latin marks possible and counterfactual situations with a subjunctive verb.

The condition is contained in the dependent clause, called the *protasis*. It is marked by the word **sī**, meaning *if* (for the negative, *unless*, Latin uses **nisi**). The independent clause is called the *apodosis*. The combination of moods and tenses in the clauses of a conditional sentence indicates which type of condition it is.

Conditions using the indicative mood

These conditions are simple to understand and translate, because they deal in concrete realities.

Past real

PROTASIS	APODOSIS
sī + Any past-tense indicative verb	Any past-tense indicative verb
Sī id fēcit, *If he did it,*	peccāvit. *he made a mistake.*

Present real

PROTASIS	APODOSIS
sī + A present-tense indicative verb	A present-tense indicative verb
Sī id facit, *If he is doing it,*	peccat. *he is making a mistake.*

Future real

PROTASIS	APODOSIS
sī + A future-tense indicative verb	A future-tense indicative verb
Sī id faciet, *If he does / will do it,*	peccābit. *he will make a mistake.*

Translate each of the following sentences into English.

1. Sī verbīs certāmus, aliī fugiunt.

_____

2. Sī id ōrābis, tē līberābō.

_____

3. Nisi amīcus meus erat, eum nōn iūvī.

_____

4. Sī mala vōbīs accidērunt, ea sustinuistis.

_____

5. Sī duo nascentur, duōs fīliōs illa habēbit.

_____

6. Nisi mēcum veniet, sōla discēdam.

_____

7. Sī mollis dominus est, servī nōn eum metuunt.

_____

8. Sī lex additur, crīmina quoque crescunt.

_____

9. Nisi trāditī sunt, relictī sunt intrā mūrōs.

_____

10. Sī nimium patiar, statim peream.

_____

Conditions using the subjunctive mood

A counterfactual condition indicates that an event did not occur or is not occurring because the condition is unfulfilled. Future events are always merely possible, but an ideal condition emphasizes the uncertainty of that possibility.

Past counterfactual

PROTASIS	APODOSIS
sī + A pluperfect-tense subjunctive verb	A pluperfect-tense subjunctive verb
Sī id fēcisset,	peccāvisset.
If he had done it,	*he would have made a mistake.*

Present counterfactual

PROTASIS	APODOSIS
sī + An imperfect-tense subjunctive verb	An imperfect-tense subjunctive verb
Sī id faceret, *If he were doing it,*	peccāret. *he would be making a mistake.*

Future ideal

PROTASIS	APODOSIS
sī + A present-tense subjunctive verb	A present-tense subjunctive verb
Sī id faciat, *If he should do it,*	peccet. *he would make a mistake.*

EXERCISE 40·2

Identify the type of condition in each of the following sentences, then translate the sentence into English.

1. Sī vēra dixissēs, tibi crēdissem.

2. Sī tergum custōs praebēret, ea ē domō ēriperētur.

3. Sī volāre possīmus, ventōs placidōs optēmus.

4. Sī duōs parentēs āmīsissēs, culpa tua fuisset.

5. Sī litterās accipiunt, forsitan eās legunt.

6. Sī mihi praecēpisset, multa certa scīvissem.

7. Sī ā caelestibus iūrābitur, prō certō id facient.

8. Sī pectora īrā rumperentur, multa illīs vulnera consequerentur.

9. Sī deus mihi parceret, magis ab hospitibus colerētur.

10. Sī eum in vinculīs retineant, illōs contemnāmus.

Indirect questions

Sometimes a question is embedded in a larger sentence but not quoted directly. This is called an indirect question, and Latin marks the dependent clause that contains the indirect question with a subjunctive verb. The verb in the independent clause usually expresses speaking, thinking, sensing, or other mental action, and the indirect question clause itself is introduced by a question word. For example:

DIRECT QUESTION	INDIRECT QUESTION
Cūr tristis est?	Mīror cūr tristis sit.
Why is he sad?	*I wonder why he is sad.*
Quis id laudat?	Sciunt quis id laudet.
Who is praising it?	*They know who is praising it.*

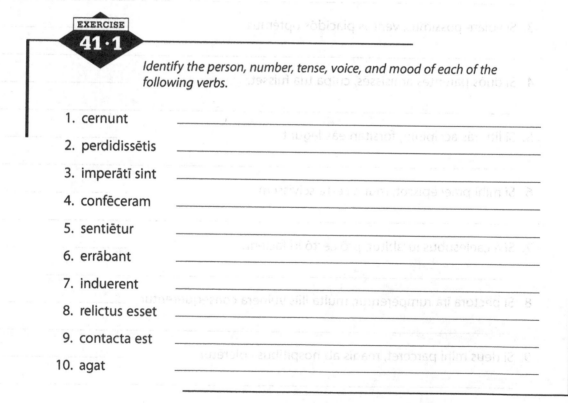

EXERCISE

41·1

Identify the person, number, tense, voice, and mood of each of the following verbs.

1. cernunt   _____

2. perdidissētis   _____

3. imperātī sint   _____

4. confēceram   _____

5. sentiētur   _____

6. errābant   _____

7. induerent   _____

8. relictus esset   _____

9. contacta est   _____

10. agat   _____

Translate each of the following sentences into English.

1. Mē rogant ubi sint aliae ovēs.

   _____

2. Meministī quem virum nōmināveris Augustum?

   _____

3. Sentiēbant quō nōs fugerēmus?

   _____

4. Quī intellegit quid respondeās?

   _____

5. Ignōrāmus quōmodo Mūsae dulcia cantent.

   _____

6. Mīrātus est quae huic accidissent.

   _____

7. Audient quārē facile fuerit loquī.

   _____

8. Dixit nōbīs quae in bellō paterētur.

   _____

9. Quaeritis cūr eōs magister nōn permittat accēdere?

   _____

10. Lēgī quās ratiōnēs prōpōnerent.

    _____

Latin-English glossary

A

ab, ā from, by
abeō, abīre, abiī, abitum go away
absum, abesse, āfuī be away
ac and
accēdō, accēdere, accessī, accessum approach
accidō, accidere, accidī happen
accipiō, accipere, accēpī, acceptum receive
ācer acris acre sharp
aciēs, aciēī (*f.*) point
ad to, toward
addō, addere, addidī, additum add
adeō, adīre, adiī, aditum approach
adhūc to this point
adsum, adesse, adfuī be present
adversus -a -um adverse
aeger aegra aegrum sick
aequor, aequoris (*n.*) sea
aequus -a -um equal
aes, aeris (*n.*) money
aetās, aetātis (*f.*) age
aeternus -a -um eternal
aethēr, aetheris (*m.*) sky
aevum, aevī (*n.*) age
afferō, afferre, attulī, allātum bring to
ager, agrī (*m.*) field
agitō, agitāre, agitāvī, agitātum pursue
agmen, agminis (*n.*) herd
agō, agere, ēgī, actum drive, act
āiō say
albus -a -um white
āles (ālitis) winged
aliēnus -a -um another's
aliquandō sometimes
aliquis aliquid someone, something
alius alia aliud other
alter altera alterum other
altus -a -um high
amīcitia, amīcitiae (*f.*) friendship
amīcus, amīcī (*m.*) friend
āmitto, āmittere, āmīsī, āmissum lose
amnis, amnis (*m.*) river
amō, amāre, amāvī, amātum love

amor, amōris (*m.*) love
an or
anima, animae (*f.*) soul
animal, animālis (*n.*) animal
animus, animī (*m.*) mind
annus, annī (*m.*) year
ante before
antīquus -a -um ancient
aperiō, aperīre, aperuī, apertum open
Apollō, Apollinis (*m.*) Apollo
appāreō, appārēre, appāruī, appāritum appear
appellō, appellāre, appellāvī, appellātum call by name
aptus -a -um fitting
apud at, at the house of
aqua, aquae (*f.*) water
arbor, arboris (*f.*) tree
ardeō, ardēre, arsī burn
argentum, argentī (*n.*) silver
arma, armōrum (*n.pl.*) weapons
armō, armāre, armāvī, armātum equip
ars, artis (*f.*) art
arvum, arvī (*n.*) field
arx, arcis (*f.*) citadel
ascendō, ascendere, ascendī, ascensum climb
aspiciō, aspicere, aspexī, aspectum look at
astrum, astrī (*n.*) star
at but
atque and
auctor, auctōris (*m.*) founder, author
audax (audācis) bold
audeō, audēre, ausus dare
audiō, audīre, audīvī, audītum hear
auferō, auferre, abstulī, ablātum carry away
augeō, augēre, auxī, auctum increase
Augustus, Augustī (*m.*) Augustus
aura, aurae (*f.*) breeze
aureus -a -um golden
auris, auris (*f.*) ear
aurum, aurī (*n.*) gold
aut or
autem however
auxilium, auxiliī (*n.*) help
avis, avis (*f.*) bird

B

Bacchus, Bacchī (*m.*) Bacchus
beātus -a -um blessed
bellum, bellī (*n.*) war
bene well
bibō, bibere, bibī drink
blandus -a -um charming
bonus -a -um good
brevis -e brief

C

cadō, cadere, cecidī, cāsum fall
caecus -a -um blind
caedēs, caedis (*f.*) slaughter
caelestis -e heavenly
caelum, caelī (*n.*) sky
Caesar, Caesaris (*m.*) Caesar
campus, campī (*m.*) plain
candidus -a -um bright
canis, canis (*m./f.*) dog
canō, canere, cecinī, cantum sing
cantō, cantāre, cantāvī, cantātum sing
cantus, cantūs (*m.*) song
capiō, capere, cēpī, captum take
caput, capitis (*n.*) head
careō, carēre, caruī, caritum lack
carmen, carminis (*n.*) song
cārus -a -um dear
castra, castrōrum (*n.pl.*) camp
castus -a -um pure
cāsus, cāsūs (*m.*) fall
causa, causae (*f.*) cause
caveō, cavēre, cāvī, cautum be careful
cēdō, cēdere, cessī, cessum go, yield
celebrō, celebrāre, celebrāvī, celebrātum honor
celer celeris celere swift
centum one hundred
cernō, cernere, crēvī, crētum discern
certō, certāre, certāvī, certātum contend
certus -a -um sure
cessō, cessāre, cessāvī, cessātum yield
cēterus -a -um other
chorus, chorī (*m.*) chorus
cibus, cibī (*m.*) food
cingō, cingere, cinxī, cinctum encircle
cinis, cineris (*m.*) ash
circā around
citus -a -um quick
cīvis, cīvis (*m./f.*) citizen
cīvitās, cīvitātis (*f.*) state
clāmor, clāmōris (*m.*) shouting
clārus -a -um famous
claudō, claudere, clausī, clausum close
coepī, coepisse, coeptum begin
cōgitō, cōgitāre, cōgitāvī, cōgitātum think
cognoscō, cognoscere, cognōvī, cognitum recognize

cōgō, cōgere, coēgī, coactum compel
cohors, cohortis (*f.*) cohort
colligō, colligere, collēgī, collectum collect
colō, colere, coluī, cultum inhabit, worship
color, colōris (*m.*) color
coma, comae (*f.*) hair
comedō, comedere, comēdī, comessum eat
comes, comitis (*m./f.*) companion
committō, committere, commīsī, commissum entrust
commūnis -e common
comparō, comparāre, comparāvī, comparātum prepare
complector, complectī, complexus embrace
compōnō, compōnere, composuī, compositum compose
concēdō, concēdere, concessī, concessum give up
condō, condere, condidī, conditum store
conferō, conferre, contulī, collātum bring together
conficiō, conficere, confēcī, confectum construct
confiteor, confitērī, confessus admit
coniunx, coniugis (*f.*) wife
cōnor, cōnārī, cōnātus attempt
consequor, consequī, consecūtus follow
consilium, consiliī (*n.*) plan
conspiciō, conspicere, conspexī, conspectum catch sight of
constituō, constituere, constituī, constitūtum establish
constō, constāre, constitī be fixed
consul, consulis (*m.*) consul
consulō, consulere, consuluī, consultum take counsel
contemnō, contemnere, contempsī, contemptum condemn
contineō, continēre, continuī, contentum contain
contingō, contingere, contigī, contactum touch
contrā against
conveniō, convenīre, convēnī, conventum come together, agree
convertō, convertere, convertī, conversum turn over
convīvium, convīviī (*n.*) party
cōpia, cōpiae (*f.*) abundance
cor, cordis (*n.*) heart
cōram in the presence of
cornū, cornūs (*n.*) horn
corpus, corporis (*n.*) body
crēdō, crēdere, crēdidī, crēditum believe
creō, creāre, creāvī, creātum create
cresco, crescere, crēvī, crētum increase
crīmen, crīminis (*n.*) charge
culpa, culpae (*f.*) fault
cum with, when, since, although
cunctus -a -um all together
cupīdō, cupīdinis (*m./f.*) desire
cupiō, cupere, cupīvī, cupītum desire
cūr why
cūra, cūrae (*f.*) concern

cūrō, cūrāre, cūrāvī, cūrātum care for
currō, currere, cucurrī, cursum run
cursus, cursūs (*m.*) race
custōdia, custōdiae (*f.*) protection
custōs, custōdis (*m./f.*) guardian

D

damnum, damnī (*n.*) loss
dē from, about
dea, deae (*f.*) goddess
dēbeō, dēbēre, dēbuī, dēbitum ought to
decet, decēre, decuit it suits
dēcipiō, dēcipere, dēcēpī, dēceptum deceive
decus, decoris (*n.*) beauty
dēdūcō, dēdūcere, dēdūxī, dēductum lead down
dēfendō, dēfendere, dēfendī, dēfensum defend
dēferō, dēferre, dētulī, dēlātum bring down
dēficiō, dēficere, dēfēcī, dēfectum lack, fail
deinde then, next
dēnique finally
densus -a -um thick
descendō, descendere, descendī, descensum climb down
dēserō, dēserere, dēseruī, dēsertum leave
dēsīderō, dēsīderāre, dēsīderāvī, dēsīderātum wish for
dēsum, dēesse, dēfuī be lacking
deus, deī (*m.*) god
dexter dextera dexterum right
dīcō, dīcere, dīxī, dictum say
diēs, diēī (*m.*) day
digitus, digitī (*m.*) finger
dignitās, dignitātis (*f.*) dignity
dignus -a -um worthy
dīligens (dīligentis) careful
dīligō, dīligere, dīlēxī, dīlectum esteem
dīmittō, dīmittere, dīmīsī, dīmissum send away
dīrigō, dīrigere, dīrēxī, dīrectum guide
discēdō, discēdere, discessī, discessum leave
discō, discere, didicī learn
diū for a long time
dīversus -a -um different
dīves (dīvitis) rich
dīvidō, dīvidere, dīvīsī, dīvīsum divide
dīvīnus -a -um divine
dīvitiae, dīvitiārum (*f.pl.*) wealth
dīvus -a -um divine
dō, dare, dedī, datum give
doceō, docēre, docuī, doctum teach
doleō, dolēre, doluī, dolitum suffer
dolor, dolōris (*m.*) pain
domina, dominae (*f.*) mistress
dominus, dominī (*m.*) master
domus, domūs (*f.*) house
dōnec until
dōnō, dōnāre, dōnāvī, dōnātum give as a gift
dōnum, dōnī (*n.*) gift

dormiō, dormīre, dormīvī, dormītum sleep
dubius -a -um doubtful
dūcō, dūcere, dūxī, ductum lead
dulcis -e sweet
dum while
duo duae duo two
dūrus -a -um hard
dux, ducis (*m.*) leader

E

ecce behold
edō, esse, ēdī, ēsum eat
efficiō, efficere, effēcī, effectum cause
ego I
ēgredior, ēgredī, ēgressus exit
ēligō, ēligere, ēlēgī, ēlectum choose
enim because
eō, īre, iī/īvī, itum go
eques, equitis (*m.*) equestrian
equus, equī (*m.*) horse
ergō therefore
ēripiō, ēripere, ēripuī, ēreptum snatch away
errō, errāre, errāvī, errātum stray
et and
etiam even
ēvādō, ēvādere, ēvāsī, ēvāsum escape
ex, ē out of, from
excipiō, excipere, excēpī, exceptum receive
exemplum, exemplī (*n.*) example
exeō, exīre, exīvī, exitum go out
exerceō, exercēre, exercuī, exercitum train
exercitus, exercitūs (*m.*) army
existimō, existimāre, existimāvī, existimātum estimate
experior, experīrī, expertus test
exspectō, exspectāre, exspectāvī, exspectātum await
extrēmus -a -um farthest

F

fābula, fābulae (*f.*) story
faciēs, faciēī (*f.*) face
facilis -e easy
faciō, facere, fēcī, factum make, do
fallō, fallere, fefellī, falsum deceive
falsus -a -um deceptive
fāma, fāmae (*f.*) reputation
famēs, famis (*f.*) hunger
famulus, famulī (*m.*) slave
fātum, fātī (*n.*) fate
fax, facis (*f.*) torch
fēlīx (fēlīcis) lucky
fēmina, fēminae (*f.*) woman
ferē nearly
ferō, ferre, tulī, lātum bring, bear
ferrum, ferrī (*n.*) iron
ferus -a -um wild
fessus -a -um tired

festus -a -um holiday
fidēlis -e faithful
fidēs, fideī (f.) faith
fīgō, fīgere, fixī, fixum fasten
fīlia, fīliae (f.) daughter
fīlius, fīliī (m.) son
fingō, fingere, finxī, finctum devise
fīnis, fīnis (m.) limit
fīō, fierī be made, become
flamma, flammae (f.) flame
fleō, flēre, flēvī, flētum weep
flōs, flōris (m.) flower
flūmen, flūminis (n.) river
fluō, fluere, fluxī, fluxum flow
foedus -a -um foul
fons, fontis (m.) fountain
foris, foris (f.) door
forma, formae (f.) beauty
forsitan perhaps
fortis -e strong
fortūna, fortūnae (f.) fortune
frangō, frangere, frēgī, fractum break
frāter, fratris (m.) brother
frequens (frequentis) crowded
frons, frontis (f.) brow
fructus, fructūs (m.) fruit
frustrā in vain
fuga, fugae (f.) fleeing
fugiō, fugere, fūgī flee
fundō, fundere, fūdī, fūsum pour
fūnus, fūneris (n.) funeral

G

Gallia, Galliae (f.) Gaul
Gallus, Gallī (m.) Gaul
gaudeō, gaudēre, gāvīsus rejoice
gaudium, gaudiī (n.) joy
gens, gentis (f.) clan
genus, generis (n.) kind
gerō, gerere, gessī, gestum carry
gignō, gignere, genuī, genitum give birth to
gladius, gladiī (m.) sword
glōria, glōriae (f.) glory
Graecus -a -um Greek
grātia, grātiae (f.) charm
grātus -a -um thankful
gravis -e heavy

H

habeō, habēre, habuī, habitum have
haud hardly
herba, herbae (f.) grass
heu alas
hic haec hoc this
hiems, hiemis (f.) winter
hinc from here

historia, historiae (f.) history
homō, hominis (m.) man
honor, honōris (m.) honor
hōra, hōrae (f.) hour
hortus, hortī (m.) garden
hospes, hospitis (m.) guest
hostis, hostis (m.) enemy
hūc to here
hūmānus -a -um civilized
humus, humī (f.) ground

I

iaceō, iacēre, iacuī, iacitum lie
iaciō, iacere, iēcī, iactum throw
iam now, already
ibi there
īdem eadem idem same
ideō for that reason
igitur therefore
ignis, ignis (m.) fire
ignōrō, ignōrāre, ignōrāvī, ignōrātum not know
ignōtus -a -um unknown
ille illa illud that
illīc there
imāgō, imāginis (f.) image
imber, imbris (m.) shower
imitor, imitārī, imitātus imitate
immensus -a -um immeasurable
imperātor, imperātōris (m.) emperor
imperium, imperiī (n.) empire
imperō, imperāre, imperāvī, imperātum order
impleō, implēre, implēvī, implētum fill
impōnō, impōnere, imposuī, impositum put onto
improbus -a -um wicked
in into, in, on
inānis -e empty
incipiō, incipere, incēpī, inceptum begin
inde from there
indicō, indicāre, indicāvī, indicātum point out
induō, induere, induī, indūtum put on
inferō, inferre, intulī, illātum bring in
inferus -a -um lower
ingenium, ingeniī (n.) talent
ingens (ingentis) huge
ingredior, ingredī, ingressus enter
inimīcus -a -um hostile
inquam say
insignis -e eminent
instituō, instituere, instituī, institūtum establish
instruō, instruere, instruxī, instructum build
integer integra integrum intact
intellegō, intellegere, intellexī, intellectum
    understand
intendō, intendere, intendī, intentum strain
inter between, among
interficiō, interficere, interfēcī, interfectum kill

interrogō, interrogāre, interrogāvī, interrogātum
   ask, question
intrā inside
intrō, intrāre, intrāvī, intrātum enter
inveniō, invenīre, invēnī, inventum discover
invideō, invidēre, invīdī, invīsum envy
ipse ipsa ipsum himself/herself/itself
īra, īrae (*f.*) anger
īrascor, īrascī, īrātus get angry
is ea id he, she, it
iste ista istud that (of yours)
ita so
Italia, Italiae (*f.*) Italy
itaque and so
item likewise
iter, itineris (*n.*) journey
iterum again
iubeō, iubēre, iussī, iussum order
iūcundus -a -um pleasant
iūdex, iūdicis (*m.*) judge
iūdicium, iūdiciī (*n.*) trial
iugum, iugī (*n.*) yoke
iungō, iungere, iunxī, iunctum join
Iuppiter, Iovis (*m.*) Jupiter
iūrō, iūrāre, iūrāvī, iūrātum swear
iūs, iūris (*n.*) law
iustus -a -um fair
iuvenis, iuvenis (*m./f.*) youth
iuvō, iuvāre, iūvī, iūtum help
iuxtā next to

L

labor, labōris (*m.*) work
labōrō, labōrāre, labōrāvī, labōrātum work
lacrima, lacrimae (*f.*) tear
lacus, lacūs (*m.*) lake
laetus -a -um cheerful
lapis, lapidis (*m.*) stone
Latīnus -a -um Latin
lātus -a -um wide
laudō, laudāre, laudāvī, laudātum praise
laus, laudis (*f.*) praise
legiō, legiōnis (*f.*) legion
legō, legere, lēgī, lectum read
leō, leōnis (*m.*) lion
levis -e light
lex, lēgis (*f.*) law
libens (libentis) willing
liber, librī (*m.*) book
līber lībera līberum free
līberō, līberāre, līberāvī, līberātum free
licet, licēre, licuit it is allowed
līmen, līminis (*n.*) threshhold
lingua, linguae (*f.*) language
linquō, linquere, līquī abandon
littera, litterae (*f.*) letter

lītus, lītoris (*n.*) shore
locus, locī (*m.*) place
longus -a -um long
loquor, loquī, locūtus speak
lūdō, lūdere, lūsī, lūsum play
lūmen, lūminis (*n.*) light
lūna, lūnae (*f.*) moon
lux, lūcis (*f.*) light

M

maestus -a -um sad
magis more
magister, magistrī (*m.*) teacher
magnitūdō, magnitūdinis (*f.*) size
magnus -a -um large
maior maius larger
mālō, malle, māluī prefer
malus -a -um bad
mandō, mandāre, mandāvī, mandātum entrust
māne early
maneō, manēre, mansī, mansum remain
manus, manūs (*f.*) hand
mare, maris (*n.*) sea
marītus, marītī (*m.*) husband
Mars, Martis (*m.*) Mars
māter, matris (*f.*) mother
māteria, māteriae (*f.*) stuff
maximus -a -um largest
medius -a -um middle
melior melius better
membrum, membrī (*n.*) limb
meminī, meminisse remember
memor (memoris) remembering
memoria, memoriae (*f.*) memory
memorō, memorāre, memorāvī, memorātum recall
mens, mentis (*f.*) mind
mensa, mensae (*f.*) table
mereō, merēre, meruī, meritum earn
metuō, metuere, metuī, metūtum fear
metus, metūs (*m.*) fear
meus -a -um my
mīles, mīlitis (*m.*) soldier
mille thousand
minister, ministrī (*m.*) attendant
minor minus smaller
mīror, mīrārī, mīrātus be amazed
mīrus -a -um wonderful
misceō, miscēre, miscuī, mixtum mix
miser misera miserum miserable
mītis -e mild
mittō, mittere, mīsī, missum send
modus, modī (*m.*) manner
moenia, moenium (*n.pl.*) walls
mollis -e soft
moneō, monēre, monuī, monitum advise
mons, montis (*m.*) mountain

mora, morae (*f.*) delay
morior, morī, mortuus die
mors, mortis (*f.*) death
mortālis -e mortal
mortuus -a -um dead
mōs, mōris (*m.*) custom
moveō, movēre, mōvī, mōtum move
mox soon
mulier, mulieris (*f.*) wife
multitūdō, multitūdinis (*f.*) multitude
multus -a -um many
mundus, mundī (*m.*) world
mundus -a -um clean
mūnus, mūneris (*n.*) service
mūrus, mūrī (*m.*) wall
Mūsa, Mūsae (*f.*) Muse
mūtō, mūtāre, mūtāvī, mūtātum change

N

nam because
namque because
narrō, narrāre, narrāvī, narrātum tell a story
nascor, nascī, nātus be born
nātūra, nātūrae (*f.*) nature
nātus, nātī (*m.*) child
nāvis, nāvis (*f.*) ship
nē *negative conjunction* (+ *subjunctive*)
-ne *indicates a question*
nec not
necessārius -a -um necessary
necessitās, necessitātis (*f.*) need
neglegō, neglegere, neglexī, neglectum disregard
negō, negāre, negāvī, negātum say not
negōtium, negōtiī (*n.*) business
nēmō, nēminis (*m./f.*) no one
nemus, nemoris (*n.*) woods
neque not
nesciō, nescīre, nescīvī, nescītum not know
niger nigra nigrum black
nihil (*n.*) nothing
nimis very much
nisi if not, unless
nix, nivis (*f.*) snow
nōbilis -e noble
noceō, nocēre, nocuī, nocitum harm
nocturnus -a -um nighttime
nōlō, nolle, nōluī not want
nōmen, nōminis (*n.*) name
nōminō, nōmināre, nōmināvī, nōminātum name
nōn not
nōs we
noscō, noscere, nōvī, nōtum know
noster nostra nostrum our
nōtus -a -um famous
novus -a -um new
nox, noctis (*f.*) night

nūdus -a -um naked
nullus -a -um none
nūmen, nūminis (*n.*) divinity
numerus, numerī (*m.*) number
numquam never
nunc now
nuntius, nuntiī (*m.*) messenger

O

ō *used with vocative to address someone or something*
ob on account of
obvius -a -um in the way
occīdō, occīdere, occīdī, occīsum kill
oculus, oculī (*m.*) eye
officium, officiī (*n.*) duty
ōlim once
omnis -e all, every
oportet, oportēre, oportuit it is proper
ops, opis (*f.*) resources
optimus -a -um best
optō, optāre, optāvī, optātum wish
opus, operis (*n.*) work
ōrātiō, ōrātiōnis (*f.*) speech
orbis, orbis (*m.*) circle
ordō, ordinis (*m.*) rank
orior, orīrī, ortus rise
ornō, ornāre, ornāvī, ornātum decorate
ōrō, ōrāre, ōrāvī, ōrātum ask for
ōs, ōris (*n.*) mouth
os, ossis (*n.*) bone
ostendō, ostendere, ostendī, ostensum show
ōtium, ōtiī (*n.*) leisure
ovis, ovis (*f.*) sheep

P

paene nearly
pandō, pandere, pandī, passum spread
pānis, pānis (*m.*) bread
pār (paris) equal
parcō, parcere, pepercī spare
parens, parentis (*m./f.*) parent
pariō, parere, peperī, partum give birth
pariter equally
parō, parāre, parāvī, parātum provide
pars, partis (*f.*) part
parum (*n.*) too little
parvus -a -um small
pateō, patēre, patuī be open
pater, patris (*m.*) father
patior, patī, passus suffer
patria, patriae (*f.*) country
paucus -a -um few
paulus -a -um small
pauper (pauperis) poor
pax, pācis (*f.*) peace
peccō, peccāre, peccāvī, peccātum make a mistake

pectus, pectoris (*n.*) chest
pecūnia, pecūniae (*f.*) money
pelagus, pelagī (*n.*) sea
pendō, pendere, pependī, pensum weigh
per through
percutiō, percutere, percussī, percussum strike
perdō, perdere, perdidī, perditum lose
pereō, perīre, periī, peritum die
perficiō, perficere, perfēcī, perfectum complete
pergō, pergere, perrexī, perrectum continue
perīculum, perīculī (*n.*) danger
permittō, permittere, permīsī, permissum allow
perpetuus -a -um continuous
perveniō, pervenīre, pervēnī, perventum arrive
pēs, pedis (*m.*) foot
petō, petere, petīvī, petītum seek
Phoebus, Phoebī (*m.*) Phoebus
pietās, pietātis (*f.*) piety
piscis, piscis (*m.*) fish
pius -a -um dutiful
placeō, placēre, placuī, placitum be pleasing
placidus -a -um calm
plēnus -a -um full
plērusque plēraque plērumque very many
plūrimus -a -um many
plūs, plūris (*n.*) more
poena, poenae (*f.*) penalty
poēta, poētae (*m.*) poet
pondus, ponderis (*n.*) weight
pōnō, pōnere, posuī, positum put
pontus, pontī (*m.*) sea
populus, populī (*m.*) people
porta, portae (*f.*) gate
portō, portāre, portāvī, portātum carry
possum, posse, potuī be able, can
post after
posteā afterwards
postquam after
postulō, postulāre, postulāvī, postulātum demand
potens (potentis) powerful
potestās, potestātis (*f.*) ability
potis -e able
praebeō, praebēre, praebuī, praebitum offer
praecipiō, praecipere, praecēpī, praeceptum teach
praecipuus -a -um special
praedīcō, praedīcere, praedixī, praedictum predict
praemium, praemiī (*n.*) reward
praesens (praesentis) present
praestō, praestāre, praestitī, praestātum excel
praeter past, alongside, besides
praetereō, praeterīre, praeteriī, praeteritum pass by
precor, precārī, precātus pray
premō, premere, pressī, pressum press
pretium, pretiī (*n.*) price
prex, precis (*f.*) prayer
prīmus -a -um first

princeps, principis (*m.*) leader
principium, principiī (*n.*) beginning
prior prius earlier
prō on behalf of
probō, probāre, probāvī, probātum approve
prōcēdō, prōcēdere, prōcessī, prōcessum advance
procul far away
prōdō, prōdere, prōdidī, prōditum give forth
proelium, proeliī (*n.*) battle
prōmittō, prōmittere, prōmīsī, prōmissum promise
prope near
properō, properāre, properāvī, properātum hurry
prōpōnō, prōpōnere, prōposuī, prōpositum propose
proprius -a -um own
propter on account of
prōsum, prōdesse, prōfuī benefit
prōtinus immediately
proximus -a -um closest
publicus -a -um public
pudor, pudōris (*m.*) modesty
puella, puellae (*f.*) girl
puer, puerī (*m.*) boy
pugna, pugnae (*f.*) fight
pugnō, pugnāre, pugnāvī, pugnātum fight
pulcher pulchra pulchrum beautiful
pūrus -a -um pure
putō, putāre, putāvī, putātum think

Q

quaerō, quaerere, quaesīvī, quaesītum seek
quālis -e what kind
quam than, how
quamquam although
quamvīs although
quandō when, because
quantus -a -um how great
quārē in what way?, why
quasi as if
quattuor four
-que and
queror, querī, questus complain
quī quae quod who, which, what
quia because
quīcumque quaecumque quodcumque whoever, whichever, whatever
quidam quaedam quoddam certain
quidem indeed
quiescō, quiescere, quiēvī, quiētum rest
quīn but that
quis quid who? what?
quisquam quicquam/quidquam any
quisque quaeque quidque each
quisquis quidquid whoever, whatever
quō where
quod because
quōmodo how

quondam once
quoniam since
quoque also

R

rapiō, rapere, rapuī, raptum snatch
rārus -a -um uncommon
ratiō, ratiōnis (*f.*) reason, account
recēdō, recēdere, recessī, recessum withdraw
recipiō, recipere, recēpī, receptum receive
rectus -a -um correct
reddō, reddere, reddidī, redditum return
redeō, redīre, rediī, reditum return
referō, referre, rettulī, relātum bring back, tell
regiō, regiōnis (*f.*) region
rēgius -a -um royal
regnō, regnāre, regnāvī, regnātum rule
regnum, regnī (*n.*) kingdom
regō, regere, rexī, rectum rule
relinquō, relinquere, relīquī, relictum leave
reliquus -a -um remaining
reperiō, reperīre, repperī, repertum discover
requīrō, requīrere, requīsīvī, requīsītum seek
rēs, reī (*f.*) thing
respiciō, respicere, respexī, respectum look back
respondeō, respondēre, respondī, responsum answer
retineō, retinēre, retinuī, retentum hold back
revertō, revertere, revertī, reversum turn back
revocō, revocāre, revocāvī, revocātum call back
rex, rēgis (*m.*) king
rīdeō, rīdēre, rīsī, rīsum laugh
rīpa, rīpae (*f.*) bank
rogō, rogāre, rogāvī, rogātum ask
rogus, rogī (*m.*) pyre
Rōma, Rōmae (*f.*) Rome
Rōmānus -a -um Roman
rosa, rosae (*f.*) rose
rumpō, rumpere, rūpī, ruptum break
rursus, rursum again
rūs, rūris (*n.*) farm
rusticus -a -um country

S

sacer sacra sacrum sacred
sacerdōs, sacerdōtis (*m.*) priest
saeculum, saeculī (*n.*) age
saepe often
saevus -a -um cruel
salūs, salūtis (*f.*) health
sanctus -a -um sacred
sanguis, sanguinis (*m.*) blood
sapiens (sapientis) wise
sapientia, sapientiae (*f.*) wisdom
satis enough
saxum, saxī (*n.*) rock

scelus, sceleris (*n.*) crime
scientia, scientiae (*f.*) knowledge
scīlicet of course
sciō, scīre, scīvī, scītum know
scrībō, scrībere, scripsī, scriptum write
secundus -a -um second
sēcūrus -a -um carefree
sed but
sedeō, sedēre, sēdī, sessum sit
sēdēs, sēdis (*f.*) seat
semel once
semper always
senex, senis (*m.*) old man
sensus, sensūs (*m.*) feeling
sententia, sententiae (*f.*) thought
sentiō, sentīre, sensī, sensum perceive
sepeliō, sepelīre, sepelīvī, sepultum bury
sepulcrum, sepulcrī (*n.*) tomb
sequor, sequī, secūtus follow
sermō, sermōnis (*m.*) conversation
serviō, servīre, servīvī, servītum be a slave
servō, servāre, servāvī, servātum save
servus, servī (*m.*) slave
seu or if
sī if
sīc in this way
sīcut just as
sīdus, sīderis (*n.*) star
signum, signī (*n.*) sign
silentium, silentiī (*n.*) silence
silva, silvae (*f.*) forest
similis -e similar
simul at the same time
sine without
singulus -a -um one each
sinus, sinūs (*m.*) fold
sīve or if
socius -a -um companion
sōl, sōlis (*m.*) sun
soleō, solēre, solitus be accustomed
sollicitus -a -um worried
sōlus -a -um only
solvō, solvere, solvī, solūtum loosen
somnus, somnī (*m.*) sleep
sonō, sonāre, sonuī, sonitum make a sound
soror, sorōris (*f.*) sister
sors, sortis (*f.*) fate
spargō, spargere, sparsī, sparsum sprinkle
spatium, spatiī (*n.*) space
speciēs, speciēī (*f.*) appearance
spērō, spērāre, spērāvī, spērātum hope
spēs, speī (*f.*) hope
spīritus, spīritūs (*m.*) breath
statim immediately
stella, stellae (*f.*) star
sternō, sternere, strāvī, strātum strew

stō, stāre, stetī, statum stand
studeō, studēre, studuī be eager
studium, studiī (*n.*) enthusiasm
sub under, near to
subeō, subīre, subiī, subitum go under
subitō suddenly
sublīmis -e lofty
sum, esse, fuī be
summus -a -um highest
sūmō, sūmere, sumpsī, sumptum take up
superbus -a -um haughty
superō, superāre, superāvī, superātum survive, outdo
supersum, superesse, superfuī outlive
suprā above
surgō, surgere, surrexī, surrectum rise
suscipiō, suscipere, suscēpī, susceptum take up
sustineō, sustinēre, sustinuī support
suus -a -um his/her/its/their own

T

taceō, tacēre, tacuī, tacitum be quiet
tālis -e such
tam so
tamen however
tamquam just as, as if
tandem finally
tangō, tangere, tetigī, tactum touch
tantus -a -um so great
tardus -a -um slow
tectum, tectī (*n.*) roof
tellūs, tellūris (*f.*) earth
tēlum, tēlī (*n.*) spear
templum, templī (*n.*) temple
temptō, temptāre, temptāvī, temptātum try
tempus, temporis (*n.*) time
tendō, tendere, tetendī, tentum stretch
tenebrae, tenebrārum (*f.pl.*) shadows
teneō, tenēre, tenuī, tentum hold
tener tenera tenerum tender
tergum, tergī (*n.*) back
terra, terrae (*f.*) land
tertius -a -um third
thēsaurus, thēsaurī (*m.*) treasure
timeō, timēre, timuī be afraid
timor, timōris (*m.*) fear
tollō, tollere, sustulī, sublātum lift, remove
torus, torī (*m.*) couch
tot so many
tōtus -a -um whole
trādō, trādere, trādidī, trāditum hand over
trahō, trahere, traxī, tractum drag
transeō, transīre, transīvī, transitum go across
trēs trēs tria three
tristis -e sad
triumphus, triumphī (*m.*) triumph
Trōia, Trōiae (*f.*) Troy

tū you (*sg.*)
tum then
tunc then
turba, turbae (*f.*) uproar
turpis -e foul
turris, turris (*f.*) tower
tūtus -a -um safe
tuus -a -um your, yours (*sg.*)

U

ubi where, when
ullus -a -um any
ultimus -a -um farthest
ultrā beyond
umbra, umbrae (*f.*) shade
umquam ever
unda, undae (*f.*) wave
unde from where
undique everywhere
ūniversus -a -um all together
ūnus -a -um one
urbs, urbis (*f.*) city
usque up to
ūsus, ūsūs (*m.*) use
ut *conjunction* + *subjunctive*
uterque utraque utrumque each of two
ūtilis -e useful
ūtor, ūtī, ūsus use
uxor, uxōris (*f.*) wife

V

vacō, vacāre, vacāvī, vacātum be idle
vacuus -a -um empty
vagus -a -um wandering
valdē greatly
valeō, valēre, valuī, valitum be strong
varius -a -um varied
vātēs, vātis (*m.*) prophet
-ve or
vehō, vehere, vexī, vectum carry
vel or
velut just as
veniō, venīre, vēnī, ventum come
ventus, ventī (*m.*) wind
Venus, Veneris (*f.*) Venus
vēr, vēris (*n.*) spring
verbum, verbī (*n.*) word
vērō truly
versus, versūs (*m.*) verse
vertō, vertere, vertī, versum turn
vērus -a -um true
vester vestra vestrum your, yours (*pl.*)
vestis, vestis (*f.*) clothing
vetus (veteris) old
via, viae (*f.*) street
vīcīnus -a -um neighboring

victor, victōris (*m.*) winner
victōria, victōriae (*f.*) victory
videō, vidēre, vīdī, vīsum see
vigilō, vigilāre, vigilāvī, vigilātum stay awake
vincō, vincere, vīcī, victum conquer
vinculum, vinculī (*n.*) chain
vīnum, vīnī (*n.*) wine
vir, virī (*m.*) man
virgō, virginis (*f.*) young woman
virtūs, virtūtis (*f.*) virtue
vīs (vīr-) (*f.*) strength
vīta, vītae (*f.*) life
vitium, vitiī (*n.*) fault

vīvō, vīvere, vixī, victum live
vīvus -a -um alive
vix hardly
vocō, vocāre, vocāvī, vocātum call
volō, velle, voluī want
volō, volāre, volāvī, volātum fly
volucer volucris volucre swift
voluptās, voluptātis (*f.*) pleasure
vōs you (*pl.*)
vōtum, vōtī (*n.*) vow
vox, vōcis (*f.*) voice
vulnus, vulneris (*n.*) wound
vultus, vultūs (*m.*) face

English-Latin glossary

A

abandon linquō
ability potestās
able potis
about dē
above suprā
abundance cōpia
account ratiō
act agō
add addō
admit confiteor
advance prōcēdō
adverse adversus
advise moneō
after post, postquam
afterwards posteā
again iterum, rursus, rursum
against contrā
age aetās, aevum, saeculum
agree conveniō
alas heu
alive vīvus
all omnis
all together cunctus, ūniversus
allow permittō
alongside praeter
already iam
also quoque
although cum, quamquam, quamvīs
always semper
among inter
ancient antīquus
and ac, atque, et, -que
and so itaque
anger īra
animal animal
another's aliēnus
answer respondeō
any quisquam, ullus
Apollo Apollō
appear appāreō
appearance speciēs
approach accēdō, adeō

approve probō
army exercitus
around circā
arrive perveniō
art ars
as if quasi, tamquam
ash cinis
ask interrogō, rogō
ask for ōrō
at the house of apud
at the same time simul
attempt cōnor
attendant minister
Augustus Augustus
author auctor
await exspectō

B

Bacchus Bacchus
back tergum
bad malus
bank rīpa
battle proelium
be sum
be a slave serviō
be able possum
be accustomed soleō
be afraid timeō
be allowed licet
be amazed mīror
be away absum
be born nascor
be careful caveō
be eager studeō
be fixed cōnstō
be idle vacō
be lacking dēsum
be made fīō
be open pateō
be pleasing placeō
be present adsum
be proper oportet
be quiet taceō

be strong valeō
bear ferō
beautiful pulcher
beauty decus, forma
because cum, enim, nam, namque, quandō, quia, quod
become fīō
before ante
begin coepī, incipiō
beginning principium
behold ecce
believe crēdō
benefit prōsum
besides praeter
best optimus
better melior
between inter
beyond ultrā
bird avis
black niger
blessed beātus
blind caecus
blood sanguis
body corpus
bold audax
bone os
book liber
boy puer
bread pānis
break frangō, rumpō
breath spīritus
breeze aura
brief brevis
bright candidus
bring ferō
bring back referō
bring down dēferō
bring in inferō
bring to afferō
bring together conferō
brother frāter
brow frons
build instruō
burn ardeō
bury sepeliō
business negōtium
but at, sed
but that quīn
by ab, ā

C

Caesar Caesar
call vocō
call back revocō
call by name appellō
calm placidus

camp castra
can possum
care for cūrō
carefree sēcūrus
careful dīligens
carry gerō, portō, vehō
carry away auferō
catch sight of conspiciō
cause causa (*noun*); efficiō (*verb*)
certain quīdam
chain vinculum
change mūtō
charge crīmen
charm grātia
charming blandus
cheerful laetus
chest pectus
child nātus
choose ēligō
chorus chorus
circle orbis
citadel arx
citizen cīvis
city urbs
civilized hūmānus
clan gens
clean mundus
climb ascendō
climb down descendō
close claudō
closest proximus
clothing vestis
cohort cohors
collect colligō
color color
come veniō
come together conveniō
common commūnis
companion comes, socius
compel cōgō
complain queror
complete perficiō
compose compōnō
concern cūra
condemn contemnō
conquer vincō
construct conficiō
consul consul
contain contineō
contend certō
continue pergō
continuous perpetuus
conversation sermō
correct rectus
couch torus
country patria (*noun*); rusticus (*adjective*)

create creō
crime scelus
crowded frequens
cruel saevus
custom mōs

D

danger perīculum
dare audeō
daughter fīlia
day diēs
dead mortuus
dear cārus
death mors
deceive dēcipiō, fallō
deceptive falsus
decorate ornō
defend dēfendō
delay mora
demand postulō
desire cupīdō (*noun*); cupiō (*verb*)
devise fingō
die morior, pereō
different dīversus
dignity dignitās
discern cernō
discover inveniō, reperiō
disregard neglegō
divide dīvidō
divine dīvīnus, dīvus
divinity nūmen
do faciō
dog canis
door foris
doubtful dubius
drag trahō
drink bibō
drive agō
dutiful pius
duty officium

E

each quisque
each (of two) uterque
ear auris
earlier prior
early māne
earn mereō
earth tellūs
easy facilis
eat comedō, edō
embrace complector
eminent insignis
emperor imperātor
empire imperium
empty inānis, vacuus

encircle cingō
enemy hostis
enough satis
enter ingredior, intrō
enthusiasm studium
entrust committō, mandō
envy invideō
equal aequus, pār
equally pariter
equestrian eques
equip armō
escape ēvādō
establish constituō, instituō
esteem dīligō
estimate existimō
eternal aeternus
even etiam
ever umquam
every omnis
everywhere undique
example exemplum
excel praestō
exit ēgredior
eye oculus

F

face faciēs, vultus
fail dēficiō
fair iustus
faith fidēs
faithful fidēlis
fall cāsus (*noun*); cadō (*verb*)
famous clārus, nōtus
far away procul
farm rūs
farthest extrēmus, ultimus
fasten fīgō
fate fātum, sors
father pater
fault culpa, vitium
fear metus, timor (*noun*);
    metuō (*verb*)
feeling sensus
few paucus
field ager, arvum
fight pugna (*noun*); pugnō (*verb*)
fill impleō
finally dēnique, tandem
finger digitus
fire ignis
first prīmus
fish piscis
fitting aptus
flame flamma
flee fugiō
fleeing fuga

flow fluō
flower flōs
fly volō
fold sinus
follow consequor, sequor
food cibus
foot pēs
for a long time diū
for that reason ideō
forest silva
fortune fortūna
foul foedus, turpis
founder auctor
fountain fons
four quattuor
free līber (*adjective*); līberō (*verb*)
friend amīcus
friendship amīcitia
from ab, ā; dē; ex, ē
from here hinc
from there inde
from where unde
fruit fructus
full plēnus
funeral fūnus

G

garden hortus
gate porta
Gaul Gallia (*noun*); Gallus (*adjective*)
get angry īrascor
gift dōnum
girl puella
give dō
give as a gift dōnō
give birth to gignō, pariō
give forth prōdō
give up concēdō
glory glōria
go cēdō, eō
go across transeō
go away abeō
go out exeō
go under subeō
god deus
goddess dea
gold aurum
golden aureus
good bonus
grass herba
greatly valdē
Greek Graecus
ground humus
guardian custōs
guest hospes
guide dīrigō

H

hair coma
hand manus
hand over trādō
happen accidō
hard dūrus
hardly haud, vix
harm noceō
haughty superbus
have habeō
he, she, it is
head caput
health salūs
hear audiō
heart cor
heavenly caelestis
heavy gravis
help auxilium (*noun*); iuvō (*verb*)
herd agmen
high altus
highest summus
himself, herself, itself ipse
his/her/its/their own suus
history historia
hold teneō
hold back retineō
holiday festus
honor honor (*noun*); celebrō (*verb*)
hope spēs (*noun*); spērō (*verb*)
horn cornū
horse equus
hostile inimīcus
hour hōra
house domus
how quam, quōmodo
how great quantus
however autem, tamen
huge ingens
hunger famēs
hurry properō
husband marītus

I

I ego
if sī
if not nisi
image imāgō
imitate imitor
immeasurable immensus
immediately prōtinus, statim
in in
in the presence of cōram
in the way obvius
in this way sīc
in vain frustrā
in what way quārē

increase augeō, crescō
indeed quidem
inhabit colō
inside intrā
intact integer
into in
iron ferrum
it suits decet
Italy Italia

J

join iungō
journey iter
joy gaudium
judge iūdex
Jupiter Iuppiter
just as sīcut, tamquam, velut

K

kill interficiō, occīdō
kind genus
king rex
kingdom regnum
know noscō, sciō
knowledge scientia

L

lack careō, dēficiō
lake lacus
land terra
language lingua
large magnus
larger maior
largest maximus
Latin Latīnus
laugh rīdeō
law iūs, lex
lead dūcō
lead down dēdūcō
leader dux, princeps
learn discō
leave dēserō, discēdō, relinquō
legion legiō
leisure ōtium
letter littera
lie iaceō
life vīta
lift tollō
light lūmen, lux (*noun*); levis (*adjective*)
likewise item
limb membrum
limit fīnis
lion leō
live vīvō
lofty sublīmis
long longus

look at aspiciō
look back respiciō
loosen solvō
lose āmittō, perdō
loss damnum
love amor (*noun*); amō (*verb*)
lower inferus
lucky fēlix

M

make faciō
make a mistake peccō
make a sound sonō
man homō, vir
manner modus
many multus, plūrimus
Mars Mars
master dominus
memory memoria
messenger nuntius
middle medius
mild mītis
mind animus, mens
miserable miser
mistress domina
mix misceō
modesty pudor
money aes, pecūnia
moon lūna
more plūs (*noun*); magis (*adverb*)
mortal mortālis
mother māter
mountain mons
mouth ōs
move moveō
multitude multitūdō
Muse Mūsa
my meus

N

naked nūdus
name nōmen (*noun*); nōminō (*verb*)
nature nātūra
near prope
near to sub
nearly ferē, paene
necessary necessārius
need necessitās
neighboring vīcīnus
never numquam
new novus
next deinde
next to iuxtā
night nox
nighttime nocturnus
no one nēmō

noble nōbilis
none nullus
not nec, neque, nōn
not know ignōrō, nesciō
not want nōlō
nothing nihil
now iam, nunc
number numerus

O

of course scīlicet
offer praebeō
often saepe
old vetus
old man senex
on in
on account of ob, propter
on behalf of prō
once ōlim, quondam, semel
one each singulus
one hundred centum
one ūnus
only sōlus
open aperiō
or an, aut, -ve, vel
or if seu, sīve
order imperō, iubeō
other alius, alter, cēterus
ought to dēbeō
our noster
out of ex, ē
outdo superō
outlive supersum
own proprius

P

pain dolor
parent parens
part pars
party convīvium
pass by praetereō
past praeter
peace pax
penalty poena
people populus
perceive sentiō
perhaps forsitan
Phoebus Phoebus
piety pietās
place locus
plain campus
plan consilium
play lūdō
pleasant iūcundus
pleasure voluptās
poet poēta

point aciēs
point out indicō
poor pauper
pour fundō
powerful potens
praise laus (*noun*); laudō (*verb*)
pray precor
prayer prex
predict praedīcō
prefer mālō
prepare comparō
present praesens
press premō
price pretium
priest sacerdōs
promise prōmittō
prophet vātēs
propose prōpōnō
protection custōdia
provide parō
public pūblicus
pure castus, pūrus
pursue agitō
put pōnō
put on induō
put onto impōnō
pyre rogus

Q

question interrogō
quick citus

R

race cursus
rank ordō
read legō
reason ratiō
recall memorō
receive accipiō, excipiō, recipiō
recognize cognoscō
region regiō
rejoice gaudeō
remain maneō
remaining reliquus
remember meminī
remembering memor
remove tollō
reputation fāma
resources ops
rest quiescō
return reddō, redeō
reward praemium
rich dīves
right dexter
rise orior, surgō

river amnis, flūmen
rock saxum
Roman Rōmānus
Rome Rōma
roof tectum
rose rosa
royal rēgius
rule regnō, regō
run currō

S

sacred sacer, sanctus
sad maestus, tristis
safe tūtus
same īdem
save servō
say āiō, dīcō, inquam
say not negō
sea aequor, mare, pelagus, pontus
seat sēdēs
second secundus
see videō
seek petō, quaerō, requīrō
send mittō
send away dīmittō
service mūnus
shade umbra
shadows tenebrae
sharp ācer
sheep ovis
ship nāvis
shore lītus
shouting clāmor
show ostendō
shower imber
sick aeger
sign signum
silence silentium
silver argentum
similar similis
since cum, quoniam
sing canō, cantō
sister soror
sit sedeō
size magnitūdō
sky aethēr, caelum
slaughter caedēs
slave famulus, servus
sleep somnus (*noun*); dormiō (*verb*)
slow tardus
small parvus, paulus
smaller minor
snatch rapiō
snatch away ēripiō
snow nix
so ita, tam

so great tantus
so many tot
soft mollis
soldier mīles
someone, something aliquis
sometimes aliquandō
son fīlius
song cantus, carmen
soon mox
soul anima
space spatium
spare parcō
speak loquor
spear tēlum
special praecipuus
speech ōrātiō
spread pandō
spring vēr
sprinkle spargō
stand stō
star astrum, sīdus, stella
state cīvitās
stay awake vigilō
stone lapis
store condō
story fābula
strain intendō
stray errō
street via
strength vīs
stretch tendō
strew sternō
strike percutiō
strong fortis
stuff māteria
such tālis
suddenly subitō
suffer doleō, patior
sun sōl
support sustineō
sure certus
survive superō
swear iūrō
sweet dulcis
swift celer, volucer
sword gladius

T

table mensa
take capiō
take counsel consulō
take up sūmō, suscipiō
talent ingenium
teach doceō, praecipiō
teacher magister
tear lacrima

tell referō
tell a story narrō
temple templum
tender tener
test experior
than quam
thankful grātus
that ille
that (of yours) iste
then tum, tunc, deinde
there ibi, illīc
therefore ergō, igitur
thick densus
thing rēs
think cōgitō, putō
third tertius
this hic
thought sententia
thousand mille
three trēs
threshhold līmen
through per
throw iaciō
time tempus
tired fessus
to ad
to here hūc
to this point adhūc
tomb sepulcrum
too little parum
torch fax
touch contingō, tangō
toward ad
tower turris
train exerceō
treasure thēsaurus
tree arbor
trial iūdicium
triumph triumphus
Troy Trōia
true vērus
truly vērō
try temptō
turn vertō
turn back revertō
turn over convertō
two duo

U

uncommon rārus
under sub
understand intellegō
unknown ignōtus
unless nisi
until dōnec
up to usque

uproar turba
use ūsus (*noun*); ūtor (*verb*)
useful ūtilis

V

varied varius
Venus Venus
verse versus
very many plērusque
very much nimis
victory victōria
virtue virtūs
voice vox
vow vōtum

W

wall mūrus
walls moenia
wandering vagus
want volō
war bellum
water aqua
wave unda
we nōs
wealth dīvitiae
weapons arma
weep fleō
weigh pendō
weight pondus
well bene
what kind quālis
when cum, quandō, ubi
where quō, ubi
while dum
white albus
who, which, what quī
who? what? quis
whoever, whichever, whatever quīcumque, quisquis
whole tōtus
why cūr, quārē
wicked improbus
wide lātus
wife coniunx, mulier, uxor
wild ferus
willing libens
wind ventus
wine vīnum
winged āles
winner victor
winter hiems
wisdom sapientia
wise sapiens
wish optō
with cum
withdraw recēdō
without sine

woman fēmina
wonderful mīrus
woods nemus
word verbum
work labor, opus (*noun*); labōrō (*verb*)
world mundus
worried sollicitus
worship colō
worthy dignus
wound vulnus
write scrībō

Y

year annus
yield cēdō, cessō
yoke iugum
you tū (*sg.*), vōs (*pl.*)
young woman virgō
your, yours tuus (*sg.*), vester (*pl.*)
youth iuvenis

Answer key

Note: The translations that follow are literal; some may sound awkward or stilted.

1   The sounds of Latin • Using a dictionary

1·2
1. mi'|hi de'|cem ē|di'|de|rit qui'|dem bar'|ba|ra to'|ti|dem ac|cē'|pe|rit com'|mu|nī
2. lo|quen'|ti|um mi'|ni|mē re|pe|ri|an'|tur in|cre|pu'|e|rit au|di|en'|ti|bus as|si'|du|ē
3. dē|li|cā|tis'|si|mās cor'|po|ris me|mo|rā|tis'|si|mus ar'|bo|rum om'|ni|um i|īs'|dem
4. ra|di'|ci|bus pul|lu|lā'|re plu|vi|ā'|lī po|su'|e|rit of|fen|si|un'|cu|lās re|de|ā'|tur
5. ex|pos|tu|lā|ti|ō'|nēs ex|po'|si|tus Ci'|ce|rō a|mī|ci'|ti|ae ver'|bīs ad'|di|tum li'|brō
6. in|scrip'|tus cog'|ni|ta me|mo'|ri|ae ex|u|be|ran'|ti|a in|te'|ri|tū au|dī'|ta

1·3
1. verb, third conjugation
2. verb, third -iō conjugation
3. verb, second conjugation
4. adjective, third declension (one ending)
5. noun, second declension
6. noun, fifth declension
7. noun, third declension
8. verb, fourth conjugation
9. noun, third declension
10. noun, fourth declension
11. noun, first declension
12. noun, second declension
13. noun, fourth declension
14. noun, third declension
15. adjective, third declension (two endings)
16. noun, third declension
17. verb, first conjugation
18. adjective, first/second declension (-us -a -um)
19. adjective, third declension (two endings)
20. adjective, third declension (three endings)

2   Verbs • The present tense of first-, second-, and fourth-conjugation verbs

2·1
1. pete-
2. creā-
3. nescī-
4. cōgitā-
5. cupe-
6. iacē-
7. gere-
8. discēde-
9. tange-
10. pugnā-

2·2	1. 3 pl.	6. 3 sg.
	2. 2 sg.	7. 3 pl.
	3. 1 sg.	8. 1 pl.
	4. 2 pl.	9. 1 sg.
	5. 3 sg.	10. 2 sg.

2·3	1. praestās	6. parat
	2. fingō	7. imperātis
	3. movēmus	8. vident
	4. sentītis	9. valēs
	5. dēbet	10. revocat

2·4
1. maneō, manēs, manet, manēmus, manētis, manent
2. audiō, audīs, audit, audīmus, audītis, audiunt
3. exerceō, exercēs, exercet, exercēmus, exercētis, exercent
4. vigilō, vigilās, vigilat, vigilāmus, vigilātis, vigilant
5. caveō, cavēs, cavet, cavēmus, cavētis, cavent
6. conveniō, convenīs, convenit, convenīmus, convenītis, conveniunt
7. vocō, vocās, vocat, vocāmus, vocātis, vocant
8. certō, certās, certat, certāmus, certātis, certant
9. sepeliō, sepelīs, sepelit, sepelīmus, sepelītis, sepeliunt
10. mūtō, mūtās, mūtat, mūtāmus, mūtātis, mūtant

2·5	1. they ask for	6. he suffers
	2. you drink	7. they sleep
	3. I die	8. we fill
	4. you carry away	9. I drag
	5. he writes	10. you increase

2·6	1. armant	6. regnās
	2. reperīs	7. tenet
	3. pervenit	8. placēmus
	4. serviunt	9. iuvant
	5. merētis	10. flēs

3   The present tense of third and third -iō conjugation verbs

3·1	1. 3 sg.	6. 3 sg.
	2. 1 sg.	7. 2 sg.
	3. 2 pl.	8. 1 sg.
	4. 2 pl.	9. 3 pl.
	5. 1 sg.	10. 1 pl.

3·2	1. relinquunt	6. accipimus
	2. colitis	7. gignō
	3. metuis	8. iaciunt
	4. vertō	9. intellegunt
	5. conspicit	10. currit

3·3
1. quaerō, quaeris, quaerit, quaerimus, quaeritis, quaerunt
2. condō, condis, condit, condimus, conditis, condunt
3. legō, legis, legit, legimus, legitis, legunt
4. cadō, cadis, cadit, cadimus, caditis, cadunt
5. praecipiō, praecipis, praecipit, praecipimus, praecipitis, praecipiunt
6. ēligō, ēligis, ēligit, ēligimus, ēligitis, ēligunt
7. ēripiō, ēripis, ēripit, ēripimus, ēripitis, ēripiunt
8. iungō, iungis, iungit, iungimus, iungitis, iungunt
9. premō, premis, premit, premimus, premitis, premunt
10. pergō, pergis, pergit, pergimus, pergitis, pergunt

3·4
1. you weigh
2. they lose
3. you fasten
4. you receive
5. I discern
6. we return
7. he goes
8. they take counsel
9. you close
10. I kill

3·5
1. compōnis
2. funditis
3. rapiunt
4. dēcipimus
5. vehit
6. fluitis
7. spargō
8. petimus/quaerimus/requīrimus
9. tenditis
10. incipiō

4   Nouns • Case endings • First-declension nouns

4·1
1. nominative
2. accusative
3. accusative
4. dative
5. nominative
6. vocative
7. genitive
8. nominative
9. ablative
10. dative

4·2
1. vi-
2. turb-
3. histori-
4. amīciti-
5. fābul-
6. pugn-
7. glōri-
8. aur-
9. poēt-
10. māteri-

4·3
1. mora
2. culpās
3. patriam
4. silvae
5. comam
6. rosās
7. litterae
8. victōriās
9. scientia
10. herbae

4·4
1. Mūsās
2. fugam
3. cūrae
4. stella/stellārum/stellīs
5. portās
6. rīpa/rīpārum/rīpīs
7. memoriās
8. fēminam
9. aquae
10. fāma/fāmārum/fāmīs

1. The poets always love the Muses.
2. He is fleeing anger.
3. Troy already stands.
4. Are you constructing a road?
5. I defend life.
6. We are seeking friendships.
7. You are not praising hair.
8. The mistress often orders.
9. Nature is finally resting.
10. Now they see the stars.

5 More case endings: genitive, dative, ablative, and vocative

5·1
1. morae
2. culpīs
3. patria
4. silvae
5. comae
6. rosārum
7. litterae
8. victōriīs
9. scientiae
10. herbīs

5·2
1. genitive and dative singular; nominative and vocative plural
2. dative and ablative plural
3. ablative singular
4. accusative singular
5. dative and ablative plural
6. genitive and dative singular; nominative and vocative plural
7. genitive plural
8. accusative plural
9. ablative singular
10. accusative singular

5·3
1. Mūsa/Mūsārum/Mūsīs
2. fugae/fugā
3. cūrīs
4. stellae
5. portae
6. rīpae/rīpā
7. memoria/memoriārum/memoriīs
8. fēminae/fēminā
9. aqua/aquārum/aquīs
10. fāmās

5·4
1. vītīs
2. īrārum
3. puellam
4. mensā
5. cōpiās
6. sententiārum
7. nātūra
8. deae
9. gratiīs
10. lūnā

5·5
1. He tells stories to the woman.
2. They decorate the table with roses.
3. Knowledge gives wisdom to memory.
4. O Italy, you are hardly escaping fault!
5. Under the shade of the forests I am sleeping.
6. He sprinkles the hair with tears.
7. The anger of the goddesses makes concerns.
8. We offer our daughters to the country.
9. After victory, they snatch the money of Troy.
10. You tell a story with your tongue.

6   Personal pronouns

6·1
1. to us / by us
2. of you (pl.)
3. you (sg.) (subject)
4. me (object)
5. we (subject) / us (object)
6. to me
7. you (sg.) (object)
8. you (pl.) (subject or object)
9. to you (sg.)
10. I

6·2
1. nōs
2. tibi
3. tū
4. nōbīs
5. ego
6. vōs
7. mē
8. nōbīs
9. tē
10. mihi

6·3
1. I am not doing harm to you.
2. You are putting us in the flames.
3. What do you estimate about me?
4. The memory of you lives again.
5. The reputation of Rome is pleasing to us.
6. I, however, have a cause.
7. The land supports me.
8. From you I now seek a delay.
9. We are almost touching the moon.
10. You fear the penalty.

7   Second-declension nouns

7·1
1. puer-
2. bell-
3. ōti-
4. thēsaur-
5. terg-
6. agr-
7. nunti-
8. tor-
9. hum-
10. ministr-

7·2
1. hortum
2. verba
3. ingeniīs
4. vīnī
5. magistrum
6. rogī
7. animīs
8. locō
9. praemia
10. pontō

7·3
1. dative and ablative singular
2. dative and ablative plural
3. genitive singular; nominative and vocative plural
4. dative and ablative plural
5. accusative singular
6. vocative singular
7. nominative, accusative, and vocative plural
8. nominative singular
9. genitive singular
10. accusative singular

7·4
1. somnōs
2. amīcīs
3. oculus/ocule/oculōrum
4. vōtōrum
5. librum
6. gaudiō
7. Phoebōs
8. templum
9. numerīs
10. puerō

7·5
1. vitiōrum
2. equōs
3. imperia
4. ministrī
5. marītus
6. castrōrum
7. armīs
8. officiō
9. fīlium
10. famulōs/servōs

7·6
1. The slaves inhabit the fields.
2. You do not know the price of the sword.
3. They honor Augustus with a triumph.
4. On the land and in the sky, you do not discern the gods.
5. The people condemns your plan.
6. I am putting on yokes in the gardens.
7. Then the woman takes the food.
8. They demand the beginning of the party with a sign.
9. Are you losing weapons next to the walls?
10. If you drink wine, you have joy.

8 Noun and adjective agreement • Adjectives ending in -us -a -um

8·1
1. prīmum
2. novōrum
3. adversā
4. nōtī
5. saevae
6. maestam
7. optimīs
8. tenerōs
9. mīra
10. tardae

8·2
1. superbī saeculī
2. beātōs annōs
3. aequa pretia
4. aeternās umbrās
5. albōrum saxōrum
6. dīversō fātō
7. dīvae deae
8. pūra flamma / pūrārum flammārum / pūrīs flammīs
9. citīs ferrīs
10. cārōrum ōtiōrum

8·3
immensō deō, singulās fēminās, dūrīs regnīs, optimōrum poētārum, vīcīna terra, ūniversīs auxiliīs, bonā fortūnā, paucum damnum, malō caelō, fessīs magistrīs, dīvīnārum scientiārum, vīvus Gallus

8·4
1. vagae aurae
2. miserīs annīs
3. dignās animās
4. iucunde Bacche
5. pulchrā terrā
6. antīqua iūdicia
7. ignōtīs dōnīs
8. magnum numerum
9. dubium silentium
10. rēgiōrum negōtiōrum

8·5

1. They are filling the wide plain in the war.
2. In this way, we see the beginning of the whole age.
3. You snatch the dear gold with foul fingers.
4. With a sure plan, they discover the gates of the temple.
5. I am holding the sacred field on your behalf.
6. We are climbing down from the high walls.
7. They give vows to the intact and divine son.
8. Wealth often outdoes even public duty.
9. For that reason, I send many letters to you.
10. You are taking up cruel battles.

9   The present tense of **sum** • Predicate sentences

9·1

1. est		6. estis	
2. es		7. est	
3. sunt/est		8. est	
4. sum		9. sumus	
5. sunt		10. est	

9·2

1. equus		6. aliēna	
2. maximī		7. dubiī	
3. causa		8. regnum	
4. vērī		9. rusticus	
5. vinculum		10. Latīna	

9·3

1. Phoebus est deus Rōmae.
2. Inimīcus est.
3. Rosae sunt nostrae.
4. Auxilium est officium amīcitiae.
5. Memoriae sunt aureae.
6. Tū es puella.
7. Augustus est dominus meus.
8. Verba sunt aliquandō arma.
9. Triumphus est clārus/nōtus.
10. Nōs sumus poētae Trōiae.

9·4

1. The Greek temple is sacred.
2. The winds on the sea are calm.
3. A blind horse returns me to you.
4. The thought is famous to me.
5. The book is in the camp of the Gauls.
6. You are wicked just as slaves.
7. Are you the master?
8. We give you a new roof.
9. I am free, not a slave.
10. The fleeings are full of dangers.

10   The imperfect tense

10·1

1. no		6. no	
2. yes		7. no	
3. yes		8. yes	
4. yes		9. yes	
5. no		10. yes	

10·2
1. 3 pl. imperfect
2. 1 sg. imperfect
3. 3 sg. present
4. 3 pl. imperfect
5. 1 sg. present
6. 3 sg. imperfect
7. 2 sg. imperfect
8. 2 pl. present
9. 3 sg. imperfect
10. 1 pl. present

10·3
1. sedēbat
2. cantābant
3. comedēbās
4. gerit
5. perdēbāmus
6. sentiēbātis
7. cingunt
8. neglegēbās
9. sepeliēbat
10. vigilābāmus

10·4
1. aperiēbāmus
2. spērābātis
3. ardēbās
4. patēbant
5. sciēbat
6. errābāmus
7. monēbātis
8. veniēbam
9. appellābant
10. laudābat

10·5
1. he was offering
2. I was wishing
3. they are killing
4. you were inhabiting
5. he was not knowing
6. you are accustomed to
7. they were fighting
8. we were fastening
9. he was sparing
10. you were increasing

11 The future tense

11·1
1. 2 sg. present
2. 2 sg. future
3. 3 sg. imperfect
4. 3 sg. future
5. 1 pl. future
6. 3 pl. present
7. 3 pl. imperfect
8. 3 pl. future
9. 2 pl. future
10. 3 pl. future

11·2
1. nōminābō
2. cognoscent
3. iaciēs
4. regnābit
5. certābant
6. recipiētis
7. sustinet
8. trahēs
9. revertēbat
10. addēmus

11·3
1. āmittet
2. tendam
3. bibēmus
4. appārēbit
5. narrābunt
6. sonābimus
7. lūdent
8. iunget
9. pervenient
10. parābitis

11·4
1. they will desire
2. I was weighing
3. he will allow
4. he is pursuing
5. you will say not
6. I will sleep
7. they put on
8. you earn
9. they will carry
10. we will take counsel

11·5
1. rapiam
2. premēs
3. cūrābit
4. tangimus
5. crēdēbātis
6. perficient
7. monēbit
8. fallēbat/decipiēbat
9. exercēbunt
10. servābimus

12 The imperfect and future tenses of **sum** • The irregular verb **possum** • The present active infinitive

12·1
1. erās
2. potest
3. possumus
4. erunt
5. potes
6. erāmus
7. poterant
8. est
9. poterit
10. sunt

12·2
1. 1 sg. imperfect
2. 3 sg. imperfect
3. 2 sg. future
4. 3 sg. present
5. 3 pl. imperfect
6. 3 pl. future
7. 3 pl. present
8. 2 sg. imperfect
9. 1 sg. future
10. 3 sg. future

12·3
1. poterat, poterit
2. erant, erunt
3. erās, eris
4. poterātis, poteritis
5. poteram, poterō
6. erāmus, erimus
7. poterās, poteris
8. eram, erō
9. erat, erit
10. poterant, poterunt

12·4
1. you are able to receive
2. they are able to leave
3. he will be able to learn
4. they were able to discover
5. he is able to burn
6. you will be able to fly
7. we were able to swear
8. I am able to lead down
9. I will be able to teach
10. you will be able to live

12·5
1. Soon he will be able to arrive at the sky.
2. Finally, they are able to divide the closest fields.
3. Again, they ought to turn their backs.
4. I was daring to leave with your books.
5. How are you able to be tired?
6. I will not be able to live without you.
7. They are able to break the new chains.
8. It is not allowed for me to enter from here.
9. He is able to kill me with a spear, if you allow (it).
10. They were able to show their limbs to us.

13   Prepositions and their cases

13·1
1. without wind
2. from gold
3. toward friends
4. in shadows
5. into the place
6. from the camp
7. with horses
8. near the wall
9. on account of companions
10. through time

13·2
1. puerīs
2. tē
3. librō
4. amīcitiīs
5. imperiō
6. Italiā
7. nātum
8. iūdicium
9. terrās
10. astra

13·3
1. in Trōiam
2. dē bellō
3. cum perīculō
4. ob/propter patriam
5. sub lūnā
6. ad proelium
7. coram deum
8. apud magistrum
9. sine cūrīs
10. per campum

14   Third-declension nouns

14·1
1. mōrī
2. capita
3. duce
4. patrēs
5. lēgis
6. cīvitātum
7. dolōrēs
8. consulibus
9. aequor
10. iūdicibus

14·2
1. ablative singular
2. accusative singular
3. dative and ablative plural
4. nominative, accusative, and vocative plural
5. dative singular
6. genitive plural
7. nominative, accusative, and vocative plural
8. accusative singular
9. dative and ablative plural
10. genitive singular

14·3
1. tenerīs
2. optima
3. dūrae
4. nocturnōs
5. mīrō
6. summō
7. iustī/iustōs
8. paucā
9. aeternārum
10. ullam

14·4
1. vestem
2. cīvēs
3. montium
4. gentem
5. animālibus
6. avī/ave
7. piscēs
8. orbī
9. noctis
10. urbs

14·5
1. nominative, accusative, and vocative plural
2. ablative singular
3. dative and ablative singular
4. nominative, accusative, and vocative plural
5. dative and ablative plural
6. accusative singular
7. genitive plural
8. ablative singular
9. nominative, accusative, and vocative plural
10. nominative, genitive, and vocative singular

14·6
1. saevōrum
2. cēterus/cēterī
3. tūtīs
4. candidae/candidās
5. inimīcō
6. maesta
7. castō
8. laetum
9. malae
10. caecī/caecōs

15 Third-declension adjectives

15·1
1. fēlix
2. fortibus
3. dulcem
4. celerī
5. audācis
6. dīvitēs
7. omnibus
8. brevēs
9. tālī
10. turpī

15·2
1. ingens/ingentem
2. fidēlī
3. acrēs/acrium
4. sublīma
5. ūtilis
6. praesentēs
7. paribus
8. mortalēs/mortālium
9. tristia
10. simile

15·3 pauperem iuvenem, potens Trōia, facilī labōrī, volucrī somnō, caelestibus deīs, sapientium iūdicum, insignis animae, magnam partem, mītem patrem, gravia vōta, levēs causās, mollia opera, commūnī mundō, frequentibus populīs

15·4
1. nostrōs puerōs
2. miserā aere
3. tōtīs cohortibus
4. grātī mīlitēs
5. ingentem rūrem
6. insignēs lūcēs
7. improbī servī
8. sollicitae precī
9. bonārum vītārum
10. fēlīcibus virginibus

15·5
1. A letter was coming into my mind.
2. Your city is a country to me.
3. The camp of the enemies will contain many cohorts.
4. I am not able to hand over or accept such money.
5. O gods, you rule the human kind with penalties.
6. We are helping the sick consul with our vows.
7. The Gaul on a noble horse was in the way.
8. The wind was leading the body under the waves.
9. He will never take up new plans.
10. Then you are killing me at the party, cruel friends!

16 Fourth-declension nouns

16·1
1. cāsū
2. cornua
3. ūsūs
4. fructūs
5. exercituum
6. domum
7. vultibus
8. spīritus
9. cantuī
10. lacibus

16·2
1. dative and ablative plural
2. genitive singular; nominative, accusative, and vocative plural
3. accusative singular
4. genitive plural
5. ablative singular
6. dative singular
7. nominative and vocative singular
8. dative and ablative plural
9. genitive singular; nominative, accusative, and vocative plural
10. accusative singular

16·3
1. perpetuī/perpetuōs
2. mollium
3. nigrīs
4. superbō
5. blandō
6. aureae/aureās
7. insignem
8. facilis
9. tardī
10. magnō

16·4
1. tōtō exercitū
2. mollēs manūs
3. variōs cāsūs
4. gravī metuī
5. pulchrī vultūs
6. tālem fructum
7. longī cornūs
8. nōtō cantuī
9. nostra domus
10. lātō lacū

17 Fifth-declension nouns

17·1
1. rem
2. diēs
3. fideī
4. speī
5. aciēs
6. faciēs
7. rē
8. diem
9. speciērum
10. fidēbus

17·2
1. genitive and dative singular
2. nominative and vocative singular; nominative, accusative, and vocative plural
3. accusative singular
4. dative and ablative plural
5. ablative singular
6. nominative and vocative singular; nominative, accusative, and vocative plural
7. genitive plural
8. genitive plural
9. accusative singular
10. nominative and vocative singular; nominative, accusative, and vocative plural

17·3
1. paucam
2. vērārum
3. media/mediae/mediās
4. Latīnae
5. vīvam
6. omnī
7. potentem
8. tristem
9. quālibus
10. mortālis/mortālī

17·4
1. bonās rēs
2. caecae fideī
3. fēlīcis dieī
4. foedae speciēī
5. iucundae rēs
6. novā rē
7. nullā aciē
8. proximus diēs
9. dubiam spem
10. mīrā faciē

18 Substantive adjectives

18·1
1. bonōs
2. pauper
3. mortuae
4. sapientium
5. publicum
6. beātīs
7. maximīs
8. parēs
9. audācēs
10. gravia

18·2
1. the old
2. many (object)
3. to the sacred / with the sacred
4. to the first / with the first
5. of the ancients
6. Greeks / of the Greek
7. the swift (subject or object)
8. mine (object)
9. to the closest / with the closest
10. to the adverse / with the adverse

18·3
1. The remaining, however, were perceiving hunger.
2. The wicked man is now thinking about crime.
3. Few people are rich.
4. Because the divine advise about the dangers from water or from fire.
5. You ought to have a large soul in adverse situations.
6. No one will be similar to me.
7. The thing itself will teach us.
8. The country ones will snatch empty causes.
9. Why are we returning money to the wise?
10. And so you know our thought.

19 More uses of the ablative

19·1
1. place from which
2. means
3. description
4. specification
5. material
6. means
7. agent
8. place where
9. separation
10. means

19·2
1. Verses then were lacking art.
2. With every concern, you complete the whole thing.
3. The son will snatch the few bones of his mother from the fire.
4. I am leading others down to my cause with gifts.
5. The slave was working in the field with the greatest enthusiasm.
6. The sword is of divine iron.
7. We were throwing rocks of huge weight.
8. The soldiers of no virtue are trying to flee.
9. Why do men live in ships through their age?
10. The poets begin to contend with a soft song.

20   The perfect tense

20·1
1. exercu-
2. reddid-
3. rūp-
4. accēp-
5. praeteri-
6. fu-
7. mīs-
8. peccāv-
9. nocu-
10. ornāv-

20·2
1. 3 pl. present
2. 3 pl. imperfect
3. 3 pl. present
4. 3 sg. perfect
5. 2 sg. perfect
6. 3 sg. present
7. 3 sg. perfect
8. 1 sg. perfect
9. 3 pl. perfect
10. 3 pl. future

20·3
1. instruximus
2. colligēbant
3. expectāvistī
4. videt
5. potuērunt
6. servābunt
7. iūrāvī
8. convenit
9. genuistis
10. fēcī

20·4
1. requīsīvistī
2. lēgit
3. dēcēpērunt
4. audīvī
5. cucurrimus
6. mōvit
7. invēnistī
8. posuit
9. creāvērunt
10. timuistis

20·5
1. he prepared / he has prepared
2. we were holding
3. they will seek
4. you closed / you have closed
5. they turned over / they have turned over
6. you snatched away / you have snatched away
7. you are proposing
8. he pressed / he has pressed
9. he says
10. we opened / we have opened

20·6
1. coēgimus
2. rettulērunt
3. docēbimus
4. tulit
5. solvēbat
6. gessistis/portāvistis/vexistis
7. permittis
8. crēvit
9. errābunt
10. crescit

21 The pluperfect and future perfect tenses

21·1
1. 1 sg. imperfect
2. 3 pl. pluperfect
3. 2 sg. perfect
4. 3 pl. perfect
5. 3 pl. pluperfect
6. 3 sg. present
7. 3 sg. future
8. 1 pl. future
9. 2 sg. pluperfect
10. 2 pl. perfect

21·2
1. placueram
2. panditis
3. arserant
4. scīverat
5. sustulistis
6. volāveram
7. cecinerant
8. retinēbit
9. incēperās
10. didicerant

21·3
1. suscēperant
2. cesserās
3. responderāmus
4. spērāveram
5. cāverās
6. contempserātis
7. frēgerat
8. verterāmus
9. aperuerās
10. existimāverat

21·4
1. he had established
2. they devised / they have devised
3. you will rejoice
4. he is causing
5. we had composed
6. you had helped
7. I had chosen
8. they had deceived
9. you approved / you have approved
10. he abandoned / he has abandoned

21·5
1. ēvāserāmus
2. commīserātis
3. caruerat
4. doluerant
5. dōnāverat
6. postulāverat
7. implēverāmus
8. vēnerant
9. intulerās
10. potueram

21·6
1. 2 sg. future perfect
2. 3 sg. perfect
3. 1 sg. future perfect
4. 3 sg. future perfect
5. 2 sg. pluperfect
6. 2 pl. future perfect
7. 3 pl. future perfect
8. 2 sg. perfect
9. 1 pl. future perfect
10. 2 pl. pluperfect

21·7
1. prōdiderit
2. carēmus
3. excēperant
4. memorābam
5. quiēverint
6. duxerit
7. mandābitis
8. relinquēbat
9. praestiteris
10. percussērunt

21·8
1. ōrāverint
2. confēceris
3. iacueritis
4. dīlexerit
5. laudāveris
6. senserimus
7. pepererō
8. celebrāverimus
9. instituerint
10. habuerit

21·9
1. he will have withdrawn
2. he was fastening
3. I will not have known
4. they had laughed
5. they will write
6. they will work
7. you are showing
8. they will not have known
9. he is killing
10. we will have increased

21·10
1. dederam
2. recēperis
3. vīcit
4. pepercērunt
5. clauserimus
6. sōnāverint
7. vacuerat
8. lūdēbant
9. cinxit
10. līberābitis

22 Demonstrative pronouns

22·1
1. hic
2. illa
3. huius
4. illae
5. illum
6. hīs
7. illa
8. huic
9. hōrum
10. hunc

22·2
1. this fate
2. these minds
3. those colors
4. this face
5. that head
6. those things
7. that grass
8. these chains
9. this mistress
10. those hands

22·3
1. hae/hās
2. ea
3. illō
4. haec
5. illīs
6. eō
7. huius
8. illārum
9. huic/hōc
10. eōrum

22·4
1. hic ingens numerus
2. eīs Rōmānīs viīs
3. illam inferam deam
4. hīs mortālibus regnīs
5. illīus sublīmis lūcis
6. id simile principium
7. eum veterem sacerdōtem
8. huius caecī oculī
9. illā acrī aciē
10. id foedum ferrum

23 Reflexive pronouns and adjectives

23·1
1. Augustus took up emperor for himself.
2. They were bringing together themselves and their things into the ships.
3. Often I ask myself, "What have you done?"
4. These friends were contending among themselves.
5. Love ordered the youths to hurry to it.
6. Soon he will come with his slave.
7. The Gauls increased their walls.
8. The father put a rock on his son's pyre.
9. You teach yourself well.
10. He was not able to know his own limits.

24 Relative clauses

24·1
1. relative pronoun: whom; antecedent: girls; case: accusative
2. relative pronoun: who; antecedent: girls; case: nominative
3. relative pronoun: that; antecedent: gifts; case: accusative
4. relative pronoun: that; antecedent: colors; case: nominative
5. relative pronoun: whom; antecedent: one; case: dative
6. relative pronoun: which; antecedent: that; case: accusative
7. relative pronoun: that; antecedent: everything; case: accusative
8. relative pronoun: which; antecedent: tools; case: ablative
9. relative pronoun: who; antecedent: man; case: nominative
10. relative pronoun: which; antecedent: city; case: ablative

24·2
1. quōs, We are eating the fruits that the land gives birth to.
2. quod, I wish to hear that which he was thinking about me.
3. quōrum/quibus, The dogs finally had discovered the herds whose guardians they were.
4. quae, Behold Rome, which is the head of the world.
5. quī, He was the man who wrote such stories.
6. quibus, We are escaping these spears with which the adversaries want to kill us.
7. quī, We praised the men who do good.
8. quae, I do not know those things that the people approve.
9. quibus, Winds were striking the ships on which we are.
10. cuius, They fear too much the divine Phoebus, whose brother is Jupiter.

25 Voice • The passive voice • The present passive tense

25·1
1. docēris
2. fingitur
3. cūrāminī
4. compōnuntur
5. retineor
6. dēcipitur
7. neglegimur
8. bibuntur
9. monētur
10. nōmināris

25·2
1. sepelītur
2. requiror
3. petuntur
4. vidētur
5. vocāmur
6. conderis
7. rumpuntur
8. ornāminī
9. vincitur
10. narrantur

25·3
1. you are being written
2. he is being ordered
3. they are being sent
4. you are being approved
5. they are being added
6. I am being touched
7. it is being poured
8. you are being lifted
9. they are being moved
10. we are being sprinkled

25·4
1. Why are such great rewards being given to me?
2. All the rank is brought together in the city.
3. The day is divided into two parts.
4. It is now entrusted by me to the doubtful breezes.
5. Money is not accepted by my teacher.
6. We are being pressed by a heavy age.
7. In the limits of this city, things are ruled by the people.
8. Cruel waters are contained by these banks.
9. We are awaited by our friends.
10. The army is equipped by the leader.

26 The imperfect and future passive tenses

26·1
1. 3 pl. present passive, they are being called by name
2. 1 sg. present passive, I am esteemed
3. 2 sg. imperfect passive, you were being led
4. 3 sg. imperfect passive, he was being left
5. 3 sg. present passive, it is given
6. 3 pl. imperfect passive, they were being created
7. 3 sg. present passive, it is carried
8. 2 pl. imperfect passive, you were being had
9. 1 pl. imperfect passive, we were being promised
10. 3 sg. imperfect passive, he was being brought down

26·2
1. traheris
2. vertēbantur
3. dīcitur
4. portābāmur
5. ōrābāris
6. audiēbantur
7. vehēbātur
8. prōpōnuntur
9. parābar
10. cingēbātur

26·3
1. rapiēbar
2. ferēbātur
3. colliguntur
4. inveniēbātur
5. constituimur
6. praedīcitur
7. cognosciminī
8. edēbantur
9. sūmēbāris
10. sentītur

26·4
1. 3 pl. future passive, they will be received
2. 3 sg. imperfect passive, it was being learned
3. 1 pl. present passive, we are being established
4. 3 sg. future passive, it will be feared
5. 3 sg. future passive, it will be climbed
6. 2 pl. future passive, you will be taken up
7. 3 pl. imperfect passive, they were being closed
8. 3 sg. future passive, it will be mixed
9. 1 sg. future passive, I will be snatched away
10. 3 sg. present passive, it is being ruled

26·5
1. revocāris
2. dīrigēbantur
3. praebēbor
4. existimantur
5. convertentur
6. implēbitur
7. cōgēbāmur
8. cupientur
9. ignōrābitur
10. contemnēminī

26·6
1. iungētur
2. ostendēbātur
3. servantur
4. colēmur
5. nocēbor
6. augēbitur
7. trādēbāminī
8. āmittuntur
9. rumpētur
10. laudāberis

27 The perfect passive tense

27·1
1. 3 sg. perfect passive, he was thought
2. 2 sg. perfect passive, you were taken
3. 3 sg. future passive, he will be loosened
4. 3 pl. perfect passive, they were given birth to
5. 3 sg. perfect passive, it was caused
6. 3 pl. perfect passive, they were discovered
7. 3 pl. perfect active, they wished
8. 1 pl. perfect passive, we were known
9. 3 sg. perfect passive, she was looked at
10. 1 pl. imperfect passive, we were being moved

27·2
1. collātae sunt
2. dabor
3. perdita est
4. apertae sumus
5. clausa es
6. cōgēbantur
7. intellectae sunt
8. audīta est
9. dēdūcēbāminī
10. sumptae sunt

27·3
1. dīmissus es
2. reversus est
3. cultī sumus
4. indicātī estis
5. mandātī sunt
6. factus sum
7. cantī sunt
8. lectus est
9. impositus es
10. contactus est

27·4
1. acta sunt
2. quaesītus est
3. pensus est
4. dōnātum est
5. interrogātī sumus
6. strātī sunt
7. iactum est
8. temptāta es
9. tentus est
10. merita est

27·5
1. creātus es
2. līberābāmur
3. iussus sum
4. agitāta est
5. passum est
6. servātur
7. putātus est
8. redditī estis
9. induentur
10. accipior

28 The pluperfect passive and future perfect passive tenses • Deponent verbs

28·1
1. 3 sg. pluperfect, he had been brought to
2. 3 pl. pluperfect, they had been fastened
3. 3 sg. perfect, it has been given up
4. 1 pl. imperfect, we were being disregarded
5. 3 sg. pluperfect, it had been discovered
6. 2 pl. pluperfect, you had been believed
7. 3 pl. perfect, they have been guided
8. 2 sg. future, you will be put onto
9. 2 sg. present, you are being allowed
10. 3 pl. pluperfect, they had been put

28·2
1. trādita erant
2. āmittar
3. aspecta erāmus
4. inceptum est
5. putāta erant
6. augēbāmur
7. requīsīta erant
8. percussum erās
9. docta erātis
10. ornātum est

28·3
1. instructī erāmus
2. tractus erat
3. imperātī/iussī erātis
4. docta erat
5. optātum erat
6. tentī erant
7. victus eram
8. perfectus erat
9. dōnātī erant
10. spērātus erās

28·4
1. 3 pl. future perfect, they will have been understood
2. 1 sg. future perfect, I will have been outdone
3. 3 sg. future perfect, it will have been snatched
4. 2 sg. perfect, you have been caught sight of
5. 3 pl. pluperfect, they had been ruled
6. 1 pl. future perfect, we will have been advised
7. 3 sg. future perfect, it will have been left
8. 2 pl. future perfect, you will have been offered
9. 3 pl. future perfect, they will have been helped
10. 3 pl. pluperfect, they had been struck

28·5
1. acceptī erunt
2. audīris
3. sublātī sunt
4. sensus erit
5. passī erimus
6. miscēbātur
7. factī erunt
8. gestus erās
9. armātī eritis
10. petītī erimus

28·6
1. laudātus eris
2. postulātus erit
3. dictum erit
4. tactī sunt
5. commissī eritis
6. vertēbātur
7. iunctī erunt
8. ducta erit
9. coactī erimus
10. missus erit

28·7
1. Those things which had been sought have been provided.
2. The ground is not being taken up into the hands.
3. Has your brother spoken nothing with you?
4. New temples to Jupiter will have been established.
5. I was awaiting the leader, whose thought I always followed.
6. The messengers were being heard by everyone.
7. We are often attempting to teach him.
8. The once enemies have now been joined by friendship.
9. The wine had been poured when the Roman army arrived.
10. Suns rise and bring the day.

29 Participles

29·1

1. certantem	6. carentī
2. parientibus	7. interficientēs
3. dormientis	8. peccantibus
4. consulens	9. surgens
5. rīdentium	10. tendens

29·2

1. doctīs	6. ēsus
2. mūtātum	7. dēfensā
3. concessī	8. iūrātae
4. dēfecta	9. occīsa
5. nescītī	10. narrātīs

29·3

1. vīsūrae	6. conspectūrum
2. exercitūrī	7. fluxūrōrum
3. vectūrās	8. rogātūrus
4. amātūrō	9. cāsūrīs
5. perrectūrae	10. dēsīderātūrum

29·4

1. iubendō	6. facienda
2. putanda	7. ēvādenda
3. tangendī	8. imperandīs
4. discendum	9. ēripiendīs
5. augendā	10. temptandī

29·5
1. dative and ablative plural, m./f./n.; perfect passive
2. nominative, accusative, and vocative plural, m./f.; present active
3. genitive singular, m./n.; nominative plural, m.; future active
4. accusative singular, m./f.; present active
5. dative and ablative singular, m./n.; perfect passive
6. accusative plural, m.; perfect passive
7. accusative plural, f.; future passive
8. accusative singular, m.; nominative, accusative, and vocative singular, n.; perfect passive
9. dative and ablative plural, m./f./n.; future active
10. dative and ablative plural, m./f./n.; perfect passive

29·6
1. The vows of the armed men were not known.
2. Praises were given to the well-given-forth conversation.
3. Understanding men were able to rejoice in the four beautiful laws.
4. We are praising the king fighting the enemies.
5. This fault of writing people had already been condemned.
6. The messengers will have been sent into parts unknown.
7. All the slaves, having been called by their master, were hurrying.
8. The man and woman about to be joined sought a priest.
9. The towers have been discovered by the soldier handed over to the enemies.
10. We are holding back Bacchus about to begin the party.

30　The ablative absolute

30·1
1. sōle orientī
2. custōde vigilantī
3. duce vīvō
4. cantibus cantīs
5. dominō dēceptō
6. duōbus iunctīs
7. cibō illātō
8. aequore/mare/pelagō/pontō nōn placidō
9. mundō ignōrātō
10. lūnā crescentī

30·2
1. While you were sleeping, Bacchus appeared to us.
2. After the table was put out, all the young women come together.
3. When the words were said, the trial was completed.
4. Because the victor is about to leave, his mother will cry.
5. Because the state is defended by a few, you will soon climb the walls of this city.
6. If Mars is the leader, more bodies are strewn through the streets.
7. Although the silver was discovered, he however did not admit (it).
8. After Rome has been seen, they will owe vows to Phoebus.
9. Although the son was killed by the enemies, his parents however hope for victory.
10. Because the winds are adverse, where are you praying to go on ships?

31　Infinitives • Indirect statement

31·1
1. iacere, iacī, iacuisse, iactum esse, iactūrum esse
2. rapere, rapī, rapuisse, raptum esse, raptūrum esse
3. vehere, vehī, vexisse, vectum esse, vectūrum esse
4. cūrāre, cūrārī, cūrāvisse, cūrātum esse, cūrātūrum esse
5. sentīre, sentīrī, sensisse, sensum esse, sensūrum esse
6. certāre, certārī, certāvisse, certātum esse, certātūrum esse
7. spargere, spargī, sparsisse, sparsum esse, sparsūrum esse
8. exercēre, exercērī, exercuisse, exercitum esse, exercitūrum esse
9. ostendere, ostendī, ostendisse, ostensum esse, ostensūrum esse
10. ēligere, ēligī, ēlēgisse, ēlectum esse, ēlectūrum esse

31·2
1. Servus dīcit templum ardēre. The slave says that the temple is burning.
2. Servus dīcit exercitum pugnāvisse. The slave says that the army fought.
3. Servus dīcit sacerdōtem fuisse sanctum. The slave says that the priest was sacred.
4. Servus dīcit animālia cornua posse habēre. The slave says that animals are able to have horns.
5. Servus dīcit ōrātiōnem placitūram esse. The slave says that the speech will be pleasing.
6. Servus dīcit tē mē amāre. The slave says that you love me.
7. Servus dīcit cohortem victam esse. The slave says that the cohort was conquered.
8. Servus dīcit verba nostra esse inānia. The slave says that our words are empty.
9. Servus dīcit pācem petītam esse. The slave says that peace was sought.
10. Servus dīcit custōdēs dormīre nec vigilāre. The slave says that the guardians sleep and don't stay awake.

32　Numbers

32·1
1. trīcensimus -a -um tertius -a -um
2. vīgintī septem
3. septimus -a -um
4. prīmus -a -um
5. decem
6. quinquāgintā
7. quingentī -ae -a
8. quintus -a -um
9. quadrāgensimus -a -um secundus -a -um
10. sescentī -ae -a quadrāgintā octō

32·2
1. 30th, trīgintā
2. 18, duodēvīcensimus -a -um
3. 100, centensimus -a -um
4. 58, quinquāgensimus -a -um octāvus -a -um
5. 4, quartus -a -um
6. 93rd, nōnāgintā trēs
7. 7th, septem
8. 16, sextus -a -um decimus -a -um
9. 8th, octō
10. 56th, quinquāgintā sex

32·3
1. duo oculī
2. prīmum senem
3. quindecim diēbus
4. vīgintī saxīs
5. ūnum imperium
6. quarta hōra
7. septimō fīliō
8. vīcensimum quintum bellum
9. trium deārum
10. mille mīlitēs

33 Expressions of time

33·1
1. hīs temporibus
2. tertiō diē
3. paucīs hōrīs
4. multōs diēs
5. prīmā lūce
6. meā aetāte
7. tot hōrās
8. sequentī nocte
9. hāc hieme
10. breve tempus

33·2
1. In these times, he was our king.
2. On the closest day, he sent books to Gaul.
3. For forty nights, I stayed awake awaiting you.
4. At the same time, each was leaving his country.
5. On the fourth day, a black horse was born.
6. In our age, Rome will not be conquered.
7. Within a few hours, they saw the running messenger.
8. For many years, the city of Troy was encircled by enemies.
9. For seven hours, he was fighting under the sun.
10. For the whole day, I attempted to hear the speech.

34 Questions

34·1
1. cuius
2. quōs
3. quō
4. quid
5. quibus
6. quae
7. cuius
8. quid
9. quibus
10. quis

34·2
1. quās terrās
2. cuius iūdicis
3. quibus senibus
4. quōs fructūs
5. quod agmen
6. quō exercitū
7. quam fidem
8. cui uxorī
9. quōs versūs
10. quī numerī

34·3
1. From where did he give that reward?
2. Whose help did you send to the army?
3. To whom were they returning a holiday day?
4. Why has the public thing not been entrusted to the immortals?
5. Who established this?
6. Whom do I attempt to escape as if evil and foul?
7. How therefore will these two kinds be divided?
8. What things had they sought with a large voice?
9. Where are you at this time?
10. In what lands were you having houses?

35 Mood • The imperative mood

35·1
1. respondē
2. vidēte
3. errā
4. tacēte
5. vigilā
6. convenī
7. adde
8. surge
9. discēde
10. agite

35·2
1. gaudēte
2. manē
3. flēte
4. venī
5. lege
6. nōlī fundere
7. cane
8. nōlīte rīdēre
9. occīde
10. stāte

35·3
1. take up!
2. promise!
3. don't turn over!
4. come!
5. save!
6. don't lie!
7. know!
8. enter!
9. contend!
10. open!

36 The subjunctive mood

36·1
1. 3 pl. present subjunctive
2. 3 pl. present subjunctive
3. 2 sg. present subjunctive
4. 3 pl. present subjunctive
5. 2 pl. present subjunctive
6. 3 sg. present indicative
7. 2 sg. future indicative
8. 3 pl. present subjunctive
9. 3 sg. present indicative
10. 1 sg. present subjunctive

36·2
1. 3 sg. present subjunctive
2. 3 pl. future indicative
3. 1 pl. present subjunctive
4. 3 sg. present subjunctive
5. 2 pl. present indicative
6. 3 pl. present subjunctive
7. 2 sg. future indicative
8. 1 sg. present subjunctive
9. 3 pl. future indicative
10. 3 sg. present indicative

36·3
1. 1 sg. imperfect indicative
2. 2 sg. future indicative
3. 3 sg. imperfect subjunctive
4. 1 sg. imperfect subjunctive
5. 3 sg. imperfect subjunctive
6. 2 sg. imperfect subjunctive
7. 3 sg. present subjunctive
8. 3 pl. imperfect subjunctive
9. 1 pl. imperfect subjunctive
10. 3 pl. imperfect subjunctive

36·4
1. 2 pl. imperfect subjunctive
2. 3 pl. imperfect subjunctive
3. 1 pl. present indicative
4. 3 sg. imperfect subjunctive
5. 3 pl. present subjunctive
6. 2 sg. imperfect subjunctive
7. 1 sg. imperfect subjunctive
8. 3 sg. imperfect subjunctive
9. 2 sg. imperfect subjunctive
10. 3 pl. imperfect subjunctive

36·5
1. 2 sg. perfect indicative
2. 1 sg. perfect subjunctive
3. 3 sg. perfect indicative
4. 1 sg. pluperfect indicative
5. 1 sg. perfect indicative
6. 3 pl. perfect indicative
7. 2 sg. perfect subjunctive
8. 2 pl. perfect subjunctive
9. 3 sg. perfect subjunctive / 3 sg. future perfect indicative
10. 3 pl. perfect subjunctive / 3 pl. future perfect indicative

36·6
1. 1 sg. perfect subjunctive
2. 1 sg. pluperfect subjunctive
3. 2 sg. pluperfect indicative
4. 3 pl. pluperfect subjunctive
5. 3 pl. perfect indicative
6. 3 pl. pluperfect subjunctive
7. 3 sg. pluperfect subjunctive
8. 3 sg. perfect indicative
9. 2 sg. pluperfect subjunctive
10. 1 sg. pluperfect subjunctive

36·7
1. 3 sg. perfect indicative
2. 1 sg. perfect subjunctive
3. 3 sg. pluperfect indicative
4. 3 pl. future perfect indicative
5. 3 sg. perfect subjunctive
6. 2 pl. perfect subjunctive
7. 3 sg. perfect indicative
8. 3 sg. perfect subjunctive
9. 1 pl. perfect subjunctive
10. 3 pl. perfect subjunctive

36·8
1. 2 sg. pluperfect subjunctive
2. 3 sg. perfect subjunctive
3. 3 sg. pluperfect subjunctive
4. 3 pl. pluperfect indicative
5. 1 pl. pluperfect subjunctive
6. 1 sg. perfect indicative
7. 2 pl. pluperfect subjunctive
8. 1 sg. pluperfect subjunctive
9. 3 sg. future perfect indicative
10. 3 pl. pluperfect subjunctive

36·9
1. 3 pl. present active subjunctive
2. 3 sg. perfect passive subjunctive
3. 3 sg. perfect active subjunctive / 3 sg. future perfect active indicative
4. 1 pl. pluperfect active subjunctive
5. 3 pl. pluperfect passive subjunctive
6. 3 sg. imperfect passive indicative
7. 3 pl. imperfect active subjunctive
8. 3 pl. perfect passive indicative
9. 2 sg. perfect passive subjunctive
10. 3 pl. future active indicative

37 Independent subjunctives

37·1
1. 3 pl. present active indicative
2. 3 sg. present passive subjunctive
3. 2 sg. future passive indicative
4. 1 pl. present passive subjunctive
5. 3 pl. present active indicative
6. 2 pl. present active subjunctive
7. 3 pl. present active subjunctive
8. 2 sg. present active subjunctive
9. 3 sg. present active subjunctive
10. 3 sg. present passive indicative

37·2
1. probent
2. doceātur
3. ardeat
4. coner
5. ōrēmus
6. sit
7. caveat
8. sequāmur
9. bibam
10. currant

37·3
1. Let the man without friends save himself.
2. But let us cause the whole thing, because we began.
3. Let the soldiers train through the winter also.
4. Let the land be light on you.
5. Let me break into the temple.
6. Let him discern that he will be blessed.
7. Let them think that my faith has been provided for everything.
8. Do the stars rise at this time?
9. The weight is not supported by the water.
10. Let us boys and girls sing of the goddess.

38 Dependent subjunctives • Purpose clauses

38·1
1. 3 sg. present active indicative
2. 3 sg. present active subjunctive
3. 3 pl. imperfect passive subjunctive
4. 3 sg. present active indicative
5. 2 sg. present passive subjunctive
6. 3 pl. imperfect active subjunctive
7. 3 pl. present active subjunctive
8. 1 pl. imperfect passive subjunctive
9. 1 sg. imperfect active subjunctive
10. 3 sg. present active subjunctive

38·2
1. I am seeking the forests in order to sleep in silence.
2. He snatched the money at night so that his evil deeds would not be understood.
3. You held back true words in order that you might deceive us.
4. We are killing the enemies so the city would remain free.
5. He closes his mouth so that he wouldn't answer them.
6. Put the flowers in the middle of the table so they are able to be seen by everyone.
7. I brought you help so that we would be friends.
8. The master hurries into the fields in order to take the fleeing slaves.
9. We put her into the land so she might finally rest.
10. To receive gifts, what have the bold not done?

39 Cum-clauses

39·1
1. 1 pl. imperfect passive indicative
2. 3 pl. present active subjunctive
3. 2 pl. imperfect active subjunctive
4. 3 pl. pluperfect active indicative
5. 1 pl. perfect passive subjunctive
6. 3 sg. present active indicative
7. 3 sg. pluperfect passive subjunctive
8. 2 pl. present passive subjunctive
9. 3 pl. imperfect active indicative
10. 2 pl. perfect active indicative

39·2
1. While the soldiers were carrying on the war, the leader was ordering them.
2. Although I stayed awake the whole night, our resources however were found and stolen.
3. Although he doesn't see land, they hope however to arrive at the shores.
4. After the country man had said these things, everyone laughed.
5. Because she fears the god of the sea, she always is careful about ships.
6. After he had spoken, his voice failed.
7. When he had done this, he fled to you, expecting more.
8. Although many sons died in the battles, one however remains.
9. Because the body is burning on the pyre, the mother and sisters cry.
10. While all the listeners were quiet, you were telling a wonderful story.

40 Conditional sentences

40·1
1. If we are contending with words, the others are fleeing.
2. If you will ask for it, I will free you.
3. Unless he was my friend, I did not help him.
4. If bad things have happened to you, you supported them.
5. If two will be born, she will have two sons.
6. Unless he will come with me, I will leave alone.
7. If the master is soft, the slaves do not fear him.
8. If a law is being added, the charges also are increasing.
9. Unless they have been handed over, those left behind are inside the walls.
10. If I will suffer too much, I will immediately die.

40·2
1. past counterfactual, If you had said true things, I would have believed you.
2. present counterfactual, If the guardian were offering his back, she would be snatched away from the house.
3. future ideal, If we should be able to fly, we would wish for calm winds.
4. past counterfactual, If you had lost two parents, the fault would have been yours.
5. present real, If they are receiving letters, perhaps they are reading them.
6. past counterfactual, If he had taught me, I would have known many sure things.
7. future real, If it will be sworn by the heavenly ones, they will do it for a certainty.
8. present counterfactual, If the chests were being broken with anger, many wounds for them would be following.
9. present counterfactual, If a god were sparing me, he would be worshipped more by guests.
10. future ideal, If they should hold him in chains, we should condemn them.

41   Indirect questions

41·1
1. 3 pl. present active indicative
2. 2 pl. pluperfect active subjunctive
3. 3 pl. perfect passive subjunctive
4. 1 sg. pluperfect active indicative
5. 3 sg. future passive indicative
6. 3 pl. imperfect active indicative
7. 3 pl. imperfect active subjunctive
8. 3 sg. pluperfect passive subjunctive
9. 3 sg. perfect passive indicative
10. 3 sg. present active subjunctive

41·2
1. They are asking me where the other sheep are.
2. Do you remember which man you named Augustus?
3. Were they perceiving where we were fleeing?
4. Who understands what you are answering?
5. We don't know how the Muses sing sweet things.
6. He was amazed at what happened to this man.
7. They will hear why it was easy to speak.
8. He said to us what he suffered in war.
9. Are you asking why the teacher does not allow them to approach?
10. I read what reasons they were proposing.